Simplified

Business Math

For

Beginners

By: Dr. John Michael Lao

Website: https://smartmoneypinoy.wixsite.com/main

Facebook: https://www.facebook.com/docmayhem/

For more about this book please contact:
drjmcl77@yahoo.com

Table of Contents

Introduction to Fractions

In simplest terms, Fractions are parts of a whole. It is a way of dividing 1 whole part into component fractional parts. The most classic of example of visualizing a fraction is thru a Pizza.

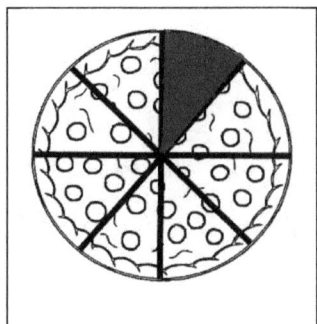	If we divide a pizza into 8 slices, a slice of pizza is consider 1 piece of an 8 pieces pizza. It is expressed as $\frac{1}{8}$ $$\frac{1 \rightarrow numerator, N}{8 \rightarrow denominator, D}$$

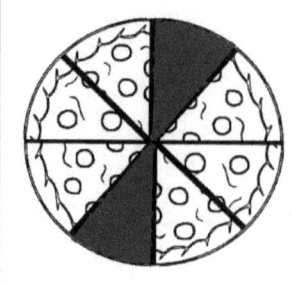

If 2 pieces of pizza are acknowledged; it will be expressed as $\frac{2}{8}$

The numerator (N) represents as the dividend and the denominator (D) represents as the divisor

It can also be presented as N ÷ D

Same as 2 ÷ 8 = 0.25 or 25%

If 4 pieces of pizza are acknowledged; it will be expressed as $\frac{4}{8}$

Same as 4 ÷ 8 = 0.5 or 50%

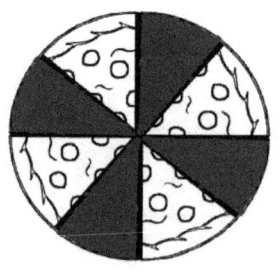

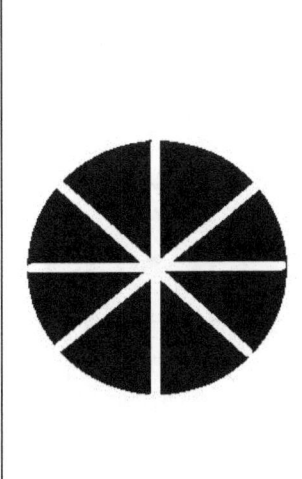	If 8 pieces of pizza are acknowledged; it will be expressed as $\frac{8}{8}$ Same as 8 ÷ 8 = 1 or 100% Hence if numerator if equal with the denominator, it is equivalent to 1

There different types of fractions that can be seen throughout mathematical equations yet only few of them are being use for business. In Table 1.1, we will explain and differentiate the types of fraction.

Table 1.1 Types of fractions

Types of fraction	Description	Example

Proper fraction	Numerator is less than the denominator. This the fraction often used in business.	$\dfrac{4}{8}$
Improper fraction	Numerator is greater than the denominator, these are seldom used in business. This type of fraction can be reduced to a mixed fraction.	$\dfrac{8}{4}$
Mixed fraction	A whole number mixed with a fraction.	$2\dfrac{1}{4}$

Equivalent fraction	Composed of 2 fraction that are of equal value. The reduced or the lowest equivalent is usually preferred for simplicity hence practicing your reduction is imperative.	$$\overset{\times 2}{\overset{\frown}{\underset{\times 2}{\underset{\smile}{\frac{1}{2}}}}} = \overset{\times 2}{\overset{\frown}{\underset{\times 2}{\underset{\smile}{\frac{2}{4}}}}} = \frac{4}{8}$$ $$\overset{\div 2}{\overset{\frown}{\underset{\div 2}{\underset{\smile}{\frac{4}{8}}}}} = \overset{\div 2}{\overset{\frown}{\underset{\div 2}{\underset{\smile}{\frac{2}{4}}}}} = \frac{1}{2}$$ $$\frac{1}{2}$$ $$\frac{2}{4}$$

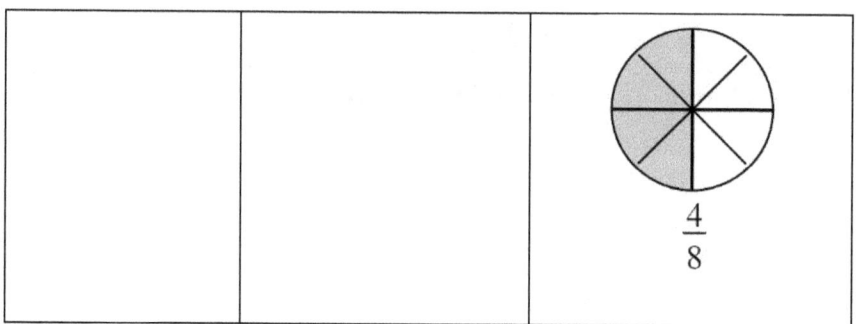

$$\frac{4}{8}$$

Post Chapter Activity #1

Topic: Introduction to Fractions

Identify the following fraction based on types of Fraction:

<blockquote>

a. Proper fraction

b. Improper fraction

c. Mixed fraction

d. Equivalent fraction

</blockquote>

1. $\dfrac{2}{4}$

2. $16\dfrac{2}{3}$

3. $\dfrac{7}{3}$

4. $1\dfrac{1}{2}$

5. $\dfrac{1}{3} = \dfrac{3}{9}$

6. $7\dfrac{2}{3}$

7. $\dfrac{20}{11}$

8. $4\dfrac{6}{7}$

9. $\dfrac{1}{2} = \dfrac{10}{20}$

10. $6\dfrac{7}{12}$

Lesson 2:

Simplifying Fractions

In fractions, the true secret in making sense of fraction is thru simplification. You have to truly simplify you fraction to make it functional for business. It will also help us understand fractions better.

Master these principles and you're on your way to become proficient at fraction.

1. Changing improper fractions to mixed fractions

Formula:

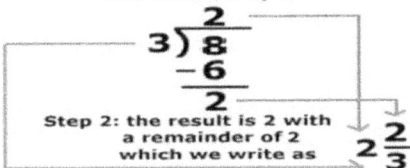

Converting Improper Fractions
to Mixed Numbers

$$\frac{8}{3} = 2\frac{2}{3}$$

Step 1: Set-up a division problem
and divide 8 by 3

```
      2
  3) 8
    -6
      2
```

Step 2: the result is 2 with
a remainder of 2
which we write as $2\frac{2}{3}$

2. Changing mixed fractions to improper fractions

Formula:

Converting Mixed Numbers
to Improper Fractions

$$2\frac{2}{3} = \frac{8}{3}$$

Step 1: multiply the whole number with
denominator then add numerator

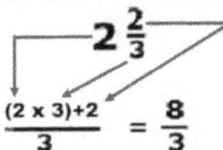

$$2\frac{2}{3}$$

$$\frac{(2 \times 3)+2}{3} = \frac{8}{3}$$

Step 2: don't change the denominator

3. Finding the equivalent fraction.

<u>Butterfly method or cross multiply method.</u> Multiply the diagonal number pair. If the answer is the same that means it is an equivalent fraction.
Example 1.

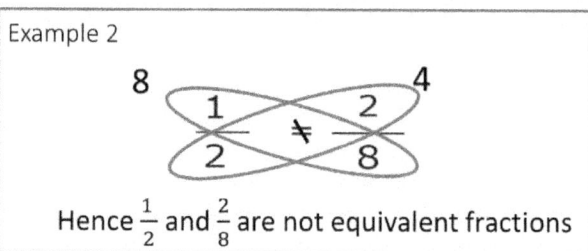

Hence $\frac{1}{2}$ and $\frac{2}{4}$ are equivalent fractions

---

Example 2

Hence $\frac{1}{2}$ and $\frac{2}{8}$ are not equivalent fractions

---

Using this principle , we can find the missing part of an equivalent fraction
Example 3.

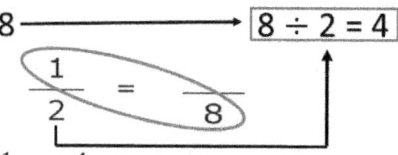

$$8 \div 2 = 4$$

Hence $\frac{1}{2}$ and $\frac{4}{8}$ are equivalent fractions

Using the same principle, we can also utilize it in comparing non-equivalent fractions

Example 4

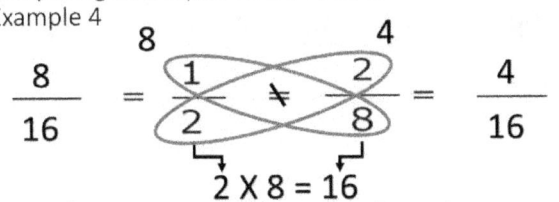

$$\frac{8}{16} = \frac{1}{2} \neq \frac{2}{8} = \frac{4}{16}$$

2 X 8 = 16

$\frac{1}{2}$ and $\frac{8}{16}$ are equivalent fractions and $\frac{2}{8}$ and $\frac{4}{16}$ are equivalent fractions hence $\boxed{\frac{1}{2}}$ is greater than $\boxed{\frac{2}{8}}$

Post Chapter Activity #2

Topic: Simplifying Fraction

Convert Improper fraction to mixed fraction:

1. $\dfrac{7}{3} =$

2. $\dfrac{11}{2} =$

3. $\dfrac{15}{5} =$

4. $\dfrac{103}{20} =$

5. $\dfrac{103}{30} =$

Convert mixed fraction to improper fraction:

6. $2\dfrac{7}{10} =$

7. $10\dfrac{1}{2} =$

8. $7\dfrac{2}{3} =$

9. $10\dfrac{1}{3} =$

10. $20\dfrac{1}{4} =$

Find the X in the Equivalent fractions

11. $\dfrac{1}{2} = \dfrac{x}{20}$

12. $\dfrac{3}{9} = \dfrac{x}{21}$

13. $\dfrac{1}{3} = \dfrac{7}{x}$

14. $\dfrac{2}{3} = \dfrac{20}{x}$

15. $\dfrac{3}{7} = \dfrac{11}{x}$

Lesson 3:

Addition and Subtraction of Fractions

In reality, fraction in business is not about the computation of the exaggeratedly large amount of number. It is not a math contest but a mastery of the different principles of basic fractions. We will explain it as simple as possible.

Basic principle of addition and subtraction of fractions

1. Addition or Subtraction of fractions with the same denominator is straightforward.

   Example: 3.1 addition and subtraction of fraction with the same denominator

Addition	subtraction
$\dfrac{4}{8} + \dfrac{4}{8} = \dfrac{8}{8} = 1$	$\dfrac{4}{8} - \dfrac{2}{8} = \dfrac{2}{8} = \dfrac{1}{4}$

$5\frac{4}{8} + 5\frac{3}{8} = 10\frac{7}{8}$	$5\frac{5}{8} - 3\frac{2}{8} = 2\frac{3}{8}$
$5\frac{4}{8} + 5\frac{4}{8} = 10\frac{8}{8}$ $= 11$	$4\frac{2}{7} - 1\frac{5}{7} = 3\frac{9}{7} - 1\frac{5}{7} = 2\frac{4}{7}$ (we can breakdown $4\frac{2}{7}$ to $3\frac{2}{7} + \frac{7}{7} = 3\frac{9}{7}$)

2. In addition or subtraction of fractions with the different denominator, we have to mathematically alter the denominator to make it the same thru looking for the **Least Common Denominator (LCD)**. The LCD of a set fraction is the least number which is a multiple of all the denominator present in the equation.

Example 3.2 addition of fractions with different denominator using the least common denominator (LCD)

Equation and solution	Process of computing for the LCD
	Since the biggest denominator is 15, we

$$\frac{4}{5} + \frac{13}{15} + \frac{11}{12} =$$

will use it to look for the least common denominator.

15 x 1 = 15

15 x 2 = 30

15 x 3 = 45

$$\frac{4+12}{5+12} + \frac{13+4}{15+4} + \frac{11+5}{12+5}$$

15 x 4 = 60

$$=$$

60 is the least number that is a multiple of all denominator (5, 15 and 12).

$$\frac{48}{60} + \frac{52}{60} + \frac{55}{60} = \frac{155}{60} =$$

$$2\frac{35}{60} = 2\frac{7}{12}$$

60 ÷ 5 = 12

60 ÷ 15 = 4

60 ÷ 12 = 5

Each quotient will be multiplied by each of the corresponding numerators.

3. Addition and subtraction fraction without using LCD. This is a different way to compute for fractions with the different denominator.

Example 3.3 addition of fractions with different denominator without using LCD

$$\frac{4}{5} + \frac{13}{15} + \frac{11}{12} =$$

Step 1 : multiply all the denominator

5 x 15 x 12 = 900 (this will be our new denominator)

Step 2 : Then divide each of the dominators from 900

900 ÷ 5 = 180

900 ÷ 15 = 60

900 ÷ 12 = 75

Step 3 : The Quotient will be multiplied with each numerator

$$\frac{4x180}{900} + \frac{13 \times 60}{900} + \frac{11x75}{900} =$$

$$\frac{720}{900} + \frac{780}{900} + \frac{825}{900} = \frac{2325}{900}$$

Step 4 : simply the fraction

$$\frac{2325}{900} \div \frac{75}{75} = \frac{31}{12}$$

Step 5 : change improper fraction to mixed fraction

$$\frac{31}{12} = 2\frac{7}{12}$$

Example 3.4 subtraction of fractions with different denominator without using LCD

$$\frac{2}{5} - \frac{1}{3} =$$

Step 1 : multiply all the denominator

5 x 3 = 15 (this will be our new denominator)

Step 2 : Then divide each of the dominators from 10

15 ÷ 5 = 3

15 ÷ 3 = 5

Step 3 : The Quotient will be multiplied with each numerator

$$\frac{2\ x\ 3}{15} - \frac{1x\ 5}{15} =$$

$$\frac{6}{15} - \frac{5}{15} = \frac{1}{15}$$

Example 3.5 subtraction of mixed fractions with different denominator without using LCD

$$2\frac{1}{4} - 1\frac{1}{3} =$$

Step 1 : change them to improper fraction

$$\frac{9}{4} - \frac{4}{3} =$$

Step 2 : multiply all the denominator

4 x 3 = 12 (this will be our new denominator)

Step 3 : Then divide each of the dominators from 12

12 ÷ 4 = 3

$12 \div 3 = 4$

Step 4 : The Quotient will be multiplied with each numerator

$$\frac{9 \times 3}{12} - \frac{4 \times 4}{12} =$$

$$\frac{27}{12} - \frac{16}{12} = \frac{11}{12}$$

Post Chapter Activity #3

Topic: Addition and Subtraction of Fraction

Perform the operation required for the Fraction:

1. $\dfrac{12}{13} - \dfrac{4}{13} =$

2. $\dfrac{5}{16} + \dfrac{3}{16} =$

3. $7\dfrac{1}{3} - 2\dfrac{1}{3} =$

4. $7\dfrac{1}{3} + 8\dfrac{1}{3} =$

5. $\dfrac{1}{4} - \dfrac{1}{5} =$

6. $\dfrac{5}{9} + \dfrac{1}{2} =$

7. $4\dfrac{1}{2} + 3\dfrac{1}{3} =$

8. $9\dfrac{1}{5} + 7\dfrac{1}{7} =$

9. $4\dfrac{1}{3} - 1\dfrac{2}{5} =$

10. $7\dfrac{1}{8} - 1\dfrac{1}{4} =$

Lesson 4:

Multiplication and Division of Fractions

Multiplication and division are straightforward regardless of difference in the denominator. You just need to follow and remember the following principles and steps and you will be on your way to mastering fractions.

Principle 1. A whole number is the same as $\dfrac{whole\ number}{1}$

Example:

$5 = \dfrac{5}{1}$	$4 = \dfrac{4}{1}$	$10 = \dfrac{10}{1}$
$23 = \dfrac{23}{1}$	$88 = \dfrac{88}{1}$	$33 = \dfrac{33}{1}$

Principle 2. Multiplication is the reverse of division.

Example:

$\dfrac{5}{1} \div \dfrac{2}{13} = \dfrac{5}{1} \times \dfrac{13}{2}$	$\dfrac{1}{12} \div \dfrac{2}{5} = \dfrac{1}{12} \times \dfrac{5}{2}$	$\dfrac{54}{17} \div \dfrac{2}{7} \div \dfrac{2}{5} = \dfrac{54}{17} \times$ $\dfrac{7}{2} \times \dfrac{5}{2}$

Principle 3. Change mixed fraction into improper fraction

Example:

$\dfrac{5}{1} \times 5\dfrac{2}{13} = \dfrac{5}{1} \times$ $\dfrac{67}{13}$	$\dfrac{1}{12} \div 2\dfrac{2}{5} = \dfrac{1}{12} \div$ $\dfrac{12}{5} = \dfrac{1}{12} \times \dfrac{5}{12}$	$5\dfrac{1}{7} \div 5\dfrac{2}{7} = \dfrac{36}{7}$ $\times \dfrac{7}{37}$

Principle 4. Simplify your fractions

Example:

$$5\dfrac{1}{7} \div 5\dfrac{2}{7} = \dfrac{36}{7} \div \dfrac{37}{7} = \dfrac{36}{\cancel{7}^{1}} \times \dfrac{\cancel{7}^{1}}{37} = \dfrac{36}{1} \times \dfrac{1}{37} = \boxed{\dfrac{36}{37}}$$

Principle 5. Multiply the all the denominator together followed by the numerator.

$$\frac{54}{17} \div \frac{2}{7} \div \frac{2}{5} = \frac{54}{17} \times \frac{7}{2} \times \frac{5}{2} = \frac{1890}{68} = 27\frac{54}{68} = 27\frac{27}{34}$$

Principle 6. For Multiple operations of fractions, you should remember the acronym <u>PEDMAS</u> (Parenthesis, Exponentials, Division and Multiplication from left the right and finally, Addition and Subtraction). Multiple operations should follow the PEDMAS PRINCIPLE in order to come up with the right answer.

Example:

$$(\frac{1}{4})^3 \div (\frac{1}{8})^2 - \frac{1}{6} = (\frac{1}{4} \times \frac{1}{4} \times \frac{1}{4}) \div (\frac{1}{8} \times \frac{1}{8}) - \frac{1}{6} = \frac{1}{64} \div \frac{1}{64} - \frac{1}{6} =$$

$$\frac{1}{64} \times \frac{64}{1} - \frac{1}{6} = 1 - \frac{1}{6} = \frac{6}{6} - \frac{1}{6} = \boxed{\frac{5}{6}}$$

$$\frac{3}{8} \div \frac{2}{3} + \frac{2}{3} \times 3 = \frac{3}{8} \times \frac{3}{2} + \frac{2}{3} \times 3 =$$

$$\frac{9}{16} + \frac{2}{3} \times \frac{3}{1} = \frac{9}{16} + \frac{2}{1} \times \frac{1}{1} =$$

$$\frac{9}{16} + \frac{2}{1} = \frac{9}{16} + \frac{2}{1} = \frac{9+2(16)}{16} = \frac{41}{16} =$$

$$2\frac{9}{16}$$

Post Chapter Activity #4

Topic: multiplication and division of Fraction

Answer the Questions:

1. $\frac{3}{4} x \frac{1}{7} =$

2. $\frac{1}{2} x \frac{1}{4} =$

3. $\frac{3}{4} \div \frac{1}{7} =$

4. $\frac{1}{2} \div \frac{1}{4} =$

5. $5\frac{1}{2} x 7\frac{1}{3} =$

6. $5\frac{1}{2} \div 7\frac{1}{3} =$

7. $5\frac{1}{2} \div 7\frac{2}{3} x \frac{5}{7} =$

8. $5\frac{1}{2} \div 7\frac{2}{3} \div \frac{5}{7} =$

9. $1\frac{1}{2} \div 3\frac{1}{4} \div 5\frac{1}{5} =$

10. $7\frac{1}{2} \div 10\frac{1}{4} \div 11 =$

Decimals and Percentage

Decimals are any number in our base-ten number system or any number on the right side of the decimal point. We are familiar with decimals more particularly with money for it represents cents (e.g. ₱ 10.75).

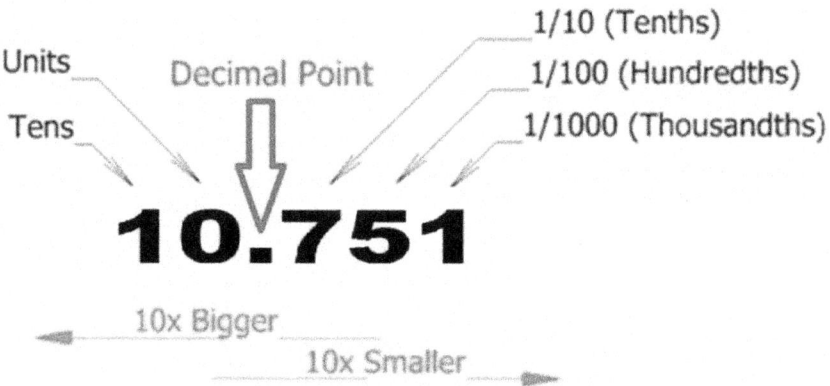

PLACE VALUE AND DECIMALS

millions	hundred thousands	ten thousands	thousands	hundreds	tens	ones	and	tenths	hundredths	thousandths	ten-thousandths	hundred-thousandths	millionths
					1	2	·	6	7				

A <u>Percentage</u> is a number expressed as a fraction of 100. It is often used in business to visualize and understand a number as a part of 100 parts. We use % as its symbol.

Example. 25% means 25 parts of 100 parts

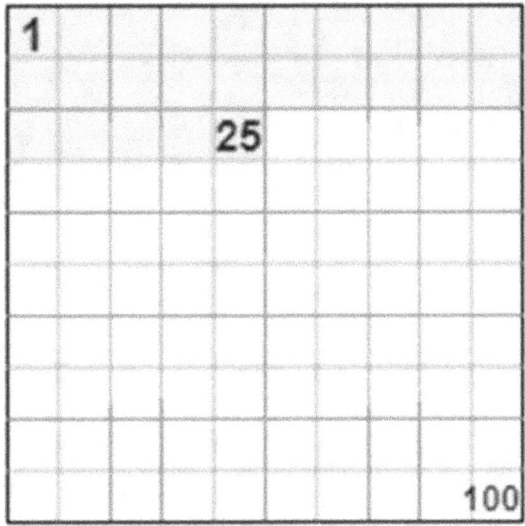

Why is it important?

We usually interchange fractions, decimals, and percentage on a regular basis in business, hence master of interchanging each is an important part of business math.

Post Chapter Activity #4

Topic: Decimal and Percentage

Convert decimal to percentage:

1. 0.7 =
2. 2.3 =
3. 0.04 =
4. 10.5 =
5. 0.111 =

Convert percentage to decimal:

1. 7% =
2. 21% =
3. 2% =
4. 55%=
5. 66.7% =

Interchanging Fraction, Decimal, and Percentage

Interchanging between Fractions, Decimals, and Percentage is essential for business mathematics. In business, we usually use fraction and percentage to illustrate and define parts of a whole like company share or ingredients of a recipe, while decimals are commonly seen in measurements and currencies. The interchanging of these elements are important and the principle behind will be explained thru the examples below.

INTERCHANGING FRACTIONS TO DECIMAL

$\dfrac{2}{7} = 2 \div 7 = 0.2857$	$\dfrac{4}{8} = 4 \div 8 = 0.5$
$\dfrac{1}{3} = 1 \div 3 = 0.3333$	$\dfrac{4}{5} = 4 \div 5 = 0.8$

INTERCHANGING DECIMAL TO PERCENTAGE

0.2857 X 100% = 28.57%	0.5 X 100% = 5%
0.3333 X 100% = 33.33%	0.8 X 100% = 80%

INTERCHANGING DECIMAL TO FRACTION

$$2.625 = \frac{2.625}{1} \times \frac{1000}{1000} = \frac{2625}{1000} = \frac{2625 \div 125}{1000 \div 125} = \frac{21}{8} = 2\frac{5}{8}$$

Post Chapter Activity #6

Topic: interchanging Fraction Decimal and Percentage

Convert decimal to fraction:

1. 2.25 =
2. 5.975=
3. 16.2 =
4. 7.2 =
5. 8.25 =
6. 6.2 =
7. 3.25 =
8. 7.25 =
9. 8.2 =
10. 9.5 =

Lesson 7:

Fractions, Decimals, and Percentage in Business

The process of interchanging fraction, decimals and percentage are critical in a business setting. The interplay and practical use between these elements in business will be understood better thru examples and problem-solving scenarios hence we will learn as we go thru the following examples.

Scenario #1. Three friends (ALVIN, JAMES, and BOB) are planning to make a soda distribution company. They need a capital of ₱500,000 to start the business. Alvin pledge $\frac{2}{7}$, James pledge $\frac{2}{7}$ and Bob pledge $\frac{3}{7}$. How much does this mean in percentage and currency?

Step 1. Change the ratio to percentage

ALVIN	JAMES	BOB
$\frac{2}{7} = 2 \div 7 = 0.2857$	$\frac{2}{7} = 2 \div 7 = 0.2857$	$\frac{3}{7} = 3 \div 7 = 0.42857$
0.2857 x 100% = 28.57%	0.2857 x 100% = 28.57%	0.42857 x 100% = 42.86%

Step 2. Find the percentage of each based on the capital of ₱500,000.

Multiply the decimal answer with the capital.

ALVIN	JAMES	BOB
28.57% of ₱ 500,000	28.57% of ₱ 500,000	42.86% of ₱ 500,000

0.2857 x ₱	0.2857 x ₱	0.4286 X ₱
500,000	500,000	500,000
=₱ 142,850	=₱ 142,850	=₱ 214,300

Scenario #2. Company ABZ made is trying to limit their annual expense to ₱ 760,000 per year. They allocated $\frac{1}{8}$ for operational expense, $\frac{2}{10}$ for employee's food expense, $\frac{3}{13}$ for rentals expenses, $\frac{3}{15}$ for insurance expense, $\frac{3}{15}$ for the recreational expense and the rest petty cash. How much money is allocated for each of the expenses?

Step 1. Change the ratio to percentage		
Operational expense	Employee's food	rental $\frac{3}{13} = 3 \div 13 = 0.23$

40

$\frac{1}{8} = 1 \div 8 =$ 0.125 0.125 x 100% = 12.5%	$\frac{2}{10} = 2 \div 10 = 0.2$ 0.2 x 100% = 20%	0.23 x 100% = 23%
Insurance expense $\frac{3}{15} = 3 \div 15 = 0.2$ 0.2 x 100% = 20%	Recreational expense $\frac{3}{15} = 3 \div 15 = 0.2$ 0.2 x 100% = 20%	Petty cash 100% - (12.5% +20%+23%+20%+20%) = 4.5%

Step 2. Find the percentage on each based of ₱ 760,000

Multiply the decimal answer with the total expense allocated.

Operational expense 12.5% 0.125 x ₱ 760,000 = ₱ 95,000	Employee's food 20% 0.20 x ₱ 760,000 = ₱ 152,000	rental 23% 0.23 x ₱ 760,000 = ₱ 174,800
Insurance expense 20% 0.20 x ₱ 760,000 = ₱ 152,000	Recreational expense 20% 0.20 x ₱ 760,000 = ₱ 152,000	Petty cash 4.5% 0.045 x ₱ 760,000 = ₱ 34,200

Scenario #3. Company ABZ made is a toy company that can a toy car per $2\frac{1}{4}$ hours. Last month they worked for 90 hours. How much money did they make last month if a toy was sold for ₱1,500 and $\frac{3}{4}$ of toys were sold?

Step 1. Change the conversion time of a toy to a decimal for easy computation
$2\frac{1}{4}$ hours = 2.25 hours
Step 2. Find out how many toys can be manufactured in 90 hours
90 hours x $\dfrac{1\ toy}{2.25\ hours} = \dfrac{90\ toy}{2.25} = 40$ toys
Step 4. Find out the number toys sold if only $\frac{3}{4}$ were sold last month.
40 toys x $\dfrac{3}{4}$ = 30 toys
Step 5. Convert toys sold in pesos
30 toy x $\dfrac{1,500\ pesos}{1\ toy}$ = ₱45,000

Topic: Fraction Decimal and Percentage in Business

Answer the following:

1. Mario , Sheila, and Anthony owns $\frac{3}{10}$, $\frac{2}{10}$, $\frac{5}{10}$ of a 5,000,000 company.
   Find the percentage of their ownership of the company.

   Find the actual amount of their ownership of the company.

2. **Black Belt Company made 30,000,000 net income from its different subsidiaries. The income can be divided to 70% from the karate school and 30% from Café Company. Since the Karate School is debt**

free, they will use 40% of the Café Company's income to pay its loans.

How much is the actual profit of the karate school and the Café?

How much is the loan of the Café?

How much will be the retained earnings of the café after the loan payments.

PBR method

(Percentage, Base, and Rate)

In Business

This method of computation will accelerate your business computation of discounts, markup, increase or decrease of profits, and other computation that are needed by business managers.

Formula: P = B x R

P = percentage, share, or portion of the base after rates are applied

B = base, base price, base of the computation, the original amount or the whole amount

R = rate which is always in the % form in relation to base

These are 3 parts elements of an equation. The challenge occurs when one element is missing hence we need to figure out the answer by multiplying or dividing the 2 known elements. The secret to answering the problem is identifying which is the P, B, and R.

Example:

Scenario 1.   20 is $\frac{1}{4}$ of 80 (identify the P, B, and R)

This equation is confusing. Let us make $\frac{1}{4}$ into % to make it easier. $1 \div 4 = 0.25$ or 25 %

20 = 25% of 80

P = 20

B = 80

R = 25%

Scenario 2. If Mark is to sell his coffee cups for a 20% discount on an actual price of ₱150 / piece, how much will be his total sale if he sold 500 cups?

Let us identify the known elements.

P=?

B= ₱150

R = if it is a discount you have to subtract 20% from 100% hence the R is 80%

Sold 500 cups

P= ₱150 x 80%

P = ₱120 / piece   if he sold 500 piece hence we have to multiply $\frac{120\ pesos}{1\ cup}$ X $\frac{500\ cups}{1}$ =

₱ 60,000.00 total sales

Scenario 3. James is into the Car buy and sell business. He recently bought a 2nd hand car for ₱150,000. He then fixed the car, repainted it and spend a total of ₱20,000.00. He decided to sell it with a markup of 45 %. How much money is expecting to get for the selling the car?

Markup computation

Markup is the amount added to the cost price of goods to cover for overhead and profit.

Step 1. Compute total overhead

₱150,000 (Car price) + ₱20,000.00 (repairs) = ₱170,000.00

Step 2. Compute for the mark up

P= B x R

P= 170,000 x 45%

P= ₱76,500.00

Step 3. Add the markup from the overhead

₱76,500.00 + ₱170,000 = ₱246.500.00

Scenario 4. Andrew is presently working as a manager of a restaurant. He was getting paid ₱20,000.00 / month. He works hard and diligently so the company decided to give him a salary increase of ₱25,000.00 / month. How much is the rate of his salary increase?

Rate increase computation

First compute for the salary difference

₱25,000 (present salary)- ₱20,000 (past salary) = ₱5,000.00

$P = B \times R$

$P = ₱5,000$

$B = ₱20,000$

$R = ?$

$P \div B = R$

$R = 5,000 \div 20,000$

$R = \underline{0.25 \text{ or } 25\%}$

Scenario 5. Mario is a chicken BBQ vendor in the market. Last month, his total sale was 30,000/month from chicken BBQ. This month, there were rumors about "Bird Flu virus" killing the chickens. This news affected and brought his sales by 25% down. How much is his total sale this month?

Rate decrease computation

First, try to identify what is given.
P=?
B= ₱30,000.00
R= 25%

Then, we should get the P

P= ₱30,000.00 x 25%
P= ₱7,500.00

This P = ₱7,500.00 is the difference in sales from this month to the last month.

₱ 30,000.00 - ₱ 7,500.00 = ₱22,500.00

Hence this month's sale is ₱22,500.00 which is 25% less than the sale from the previous month

Post Chapter Activity #8

Topic: PBR method

1. Mark want to buy a car from a car dealer. He is choosing between Car A and Car B. Car A is worth 700,000 Php but with 13% discount, while Car B is worth 650,000 Php with a 10% discount. Using the PBR method compute for the savings of each car.

   Mark wants to buy the cheaper car. Which car is cheaper with their corresponding discount?

2. Kevin is always buying Spanish bread worth 120 Php per dozen. The baker told him that if he buy 5 dozen,

the price will change to 110 Php per dozen. If he buys 10 dozen, the price will change to 100 Php per dozen.

What is the rate of discount if he buys 5 dozen? How much per piece of bread?

What is the rate of discount if he buys 10 dozen? How much per piece of bread?

Ratio and proportions

Ratios are comparisons of 2 numbers or 2 quantities with same unit of measure.

Example: 1 boys and 2 girls (1:2 or $\frac{1}{2}$) or 200 grams and 1000 kg (200:1000 or 1:5 or $\frac{1}{5}$)

Rates are comparisons of 2 numbers or 2 quantities with different unit of measure.

Example: 44.43 Pesos and 1 liter (44.43 pesos/liter)

Proportions are presuming statements that two ratios are equal.

Example: 1 car and 2 drivers = 2 cars and 4 drivers

$$\frac{1\ car}{2\ drivers} = \frac{2car}{4\ drivers}$$

Butterfly method or cross multiply method. Multiply the diagonal number pair. If the answer is the same that means it is an equivalent fraction.
Example 1.

Hence $\frac{1}{2}$ and $\frac{2}{4}$ are equivalent fractions

We will begin to understand the need for them as we drill our minds with some business scenarios.

Scenario #1

Gem, Steve and Kevin work for a robotics factory. Their salaries are 45,000 Php / month, 55,000 Php/month and 60,000 Php/month. Write them in ratios in the lowest term.

Answer:

45,000: 55,000: 60,000 or

9: 11: 12 (if we divide them with 5,000 to achieve the lowest form)

Scenario #2

While in their in the robotic factory, they were assigned with different working hours per day. Gem, Steve and Kevin were assigned 4 hours and 30 minutes per day, 5 hours per day and 6 hour and 15 mins per day. Write the ratio of their working hours per day.

Answer:

First convert working days into minutes.

4 hour and 30 minutes = 270 minutes

5 hours = 300 minutes

6 hours and 15 minutes =375 minutes

270: 300: 375 = 18: 12: 25 (divided by 15)

Scenario #3

The group decided to paint their robot with 2 parts of red paint and 4 parts gold paint. The total paint mixture to be used is 100 liters. How many liters is red and gold paint?

Answer:

First write the equation properly.

Red paint 2(x)   and   gold 4(x)

2(x) + 4(x) = 100 liters

6(x) =100

x = 100 ÷ 6

x = 16.67

Red paint 2(16.67) = **33.33 liters**   and Gold 4(16.67) = **66.68 liters**

Scenario #4

Mario, Jose and Jaime have a trading company. Their company will release dividends worth 500,000 pesos. The dividend ratio of Mario and Jose is 4:5 while ratio of Jose and Jaime is 9:16. What is their corresponding dividend?

Answer:

	Mario	Jose	Jaime
Ratio	4 Carry the 9 from Jose	5 9	Carry the 5 from Jose 16
(multiply)	4 x 9 =36	5 x 9 = 45	5 x 16 = 80
Add them all = **161**			
Then use this formula: N= total dividend x each ratio Total ratio	500,000 x 36 161 =**111,801.24**	500,000 x 45 161 =**139,751.55**	500,000 x 80 161 =**248,447.21**

Scenario #5

If a copper wire cost 15 pesos per 3 meters, how much will it cost to buy 18 meters?

Answer:

$$\frac{3\ meters}{15\ pesos} = \frac{18\ meters}{x}$$

3X = 18 (15)

X = 270 ÷ 3

X = **90 pesos**

Scenario #6

If the car is traveling at 40 km / hour, how far will the car go in 180 minutes? How long will it take to travel 200 km?

Answer to first question:

$$\frac{40\ km}{60\ minutes} = \frac{X}{180\ minutes}$$

X = 120 km

Answer to first question:

$$\frac{40\ km}{60\ minutes} = \frac{200km}{x}$$

X = 300 minutes or 5 hours

Post Chapter Activity #9

Topic: Ratio and Proportion

Question #1

Alvin, Alice and Ann is working for the same advertising company. Their salaries are 75000, 25000, and 30000. Write their salaries in ratio in the lowest term.

Question 2

Alvin, Alice. Ann and Anthony worked overtime in their company. Their overtime are 5 hours 15 mins, 7 hours 30 mins, and 6 hours. Write the ratio of their overtime in the lowest term.

Question 3

Andrew has a new coffee blend that he wants to release in the market. The blend contains 5 parts Arabica and 3 parts Robusta. How much Arabica and Robusta coffee beans does he need to make a 1kg blend of coffee?

Question 4

Jess, Jin and Joey have total age of 70. Jess and Jin's age ration is 2:3 while Jin and Joey's age ratio is 4:5. What are their respective ages?

Question 5

A 40 square meter condo Andrew's building cost 2 million. If the price per square meter are generally the same in the whole building, how much does it cost to buy a condo with 70 square meters?

Question 6

If a bullet train is travelling in a speed of 300 km/hour, how far (km) can it reach if you are traveling for 40 minutes?

Lesson 10:

Buying and Selling

Buying by definition is obtaining something in exchange for payment.

Selling by definition is giving or handing over something in exchange for money.

Buying and Selling is the base of the oldest type of business endeavor which is trading. It still is the most frequent type business seen in our society. In the process of trading, products we use regularly becomes accessible for consumption. The traders, who engaged in trading products, assume the monetary risk in exchange of possible profit or loss.

How do traders make money?

Traders buy a product and insert a price ***Mark up*** or ***Margin*** when selling it. This concept is essential in pricing a product.

1. MARK-UP and MARGIN

What is the difference between a Mark-up and a Margin?

If we talk about **mark-up** our base would be the _cost of the product_ and if talk about **margin** our base would be the _sales price_.

Therefore:

Mark-up is to cost of the product; while Margin is to the sales price.

Example:

Scenario 1.

Mario bought a cellphone for 1,500.00 Php then sold it for 2,000.00 Php. Compute for the Mark up (%) and Margin (%).

Answer:

Mark-up= {(price-cost) /cost} x 100%

       = {(2,000 – 1,500) / 1,500} x 100%

       = 33%

Margin= {(price-cost) /price} x 100%

      ={(2,000 – 1,500) / 2,000} x 100%

     = 25%

Scenario 2.

Melvin bought a smart television e for 100,000.00 Php then sold it for 200,000.00 Php. Compute for the Mark up (%) and Margin (%).

Answer:

Mark-up= {(price-cost) /cost} x 100%

       = {(200,000 – 100,000) / 100,000} x 100%

```
= 100%


Margin= {(price-cost) /price} x 100%

      ={(200,000 – 100,000) / 200,000} x 100%

      = 50%
```

The following points highlight the differences between the margin and markup percentages at discrete intervals:

- at a 10% margin, the markup percentage is 11.1%
- at a 20% margin, the markup percentage is 25.0%
- at a 30% margin, the markup percentage is 42.9%
- at a 40% margin, the markup percentage is 80.0%
- at a 50% margin, the markup percentage is 100.0%

2. **MARKDOWN**

What is a markdown?

Mark down is either temporary or permanent reduction of the price an item for the purpose of increasing sell, facilitating movement of slow-moving inventory, or increasing market control against competitors.

What is the formula for a Mark down?

Mark down = Old selling price – new reduced selling price

Example. Markdown

Scenario: Sam is second-hand car salesman. Most of his second car is sold instantly making all his inventory fast moving except for 1 old classic Blue Volkswagen beetle car. He has been trying to sell this car for 150,000 Php but no one seems to be interested. He decided to mark down the selling price to 130,000 Php.

Question # 1 Compute for the Mark down?

Answer: Mark down = Old selling price – new reduced selling price

Mark down = 150,000 -130,000

Mark down = 20,000

Question # 2 Compute for the Markdown rate?

Answer:

(Formula 1) Mark down rate = 100% - [(new selling price/old selling price) X 100%]

Mark down rate = 100% - [(130,000 / 150,000) X 100%]

Mark down rate = 100% - [(130,000 / 150,000) X 100%]

Mark down rate = 100% - 86.67%

Mark down rate = 13.33%

Or

(Formula 2) Mark down rate = (mark down / old price) X 100%

Mark down rate = (20,000 / 150,000) X 100%

Mark down rate = 13.33%

Post Chapter Activity #10

Topic: Buying and Selling

Question 1

Flora sells here flowers for 300 pesos / set. The cost to make a flower set is 200 pesos. How much is the Mark up and the Margin?

Question 2

Cel is selling her cellphone for 30,000 pesos. After 3 months, she decides put down the price to 25,000 pesos. How much is the Mark down and the Mark down rate?

Discount

Trade Discount

Trade discounts are the discretionary reduction on the sale price that are given by the sellers to buyers, retailers, and wholesalers in the purchase of the seller's product. Trade discount is given to attract and motivate buyers to purchase the product or to buy the product in bulk hence it will be better for the product's market entry and product's inventory momentum.

2 types Major types of trade discount:

1. Single trade discount – is a discount that is typically given one time. It is easier to compute. Formula : Discounted price = Sales price - (Sales price X discount (%))

2. Series trade discounts – are discount given by sellers in a series. Aside from the normal discount, the seller may grants a buyer additional discount. If a seller grant a buyer 15% discount then additional 5%, this is not equivalent to 20% as you will learn this in later example.

Formula:

1st Discounted price = primary sales price - (sales price X 1st discount (%))

Then

2nd Discounted price = 1st discounted price- (1st discount price X 2nd discount (%))

Example:

Scenario #1

Manny owns a bookshop. To be able to attract clients, he offers a back to school discount of 15%. Alvin one of his client bought a 1000 Php book.

Question# 1. How much is the discounted price of the book?

Answer:

1. Formula : Discounted price = Sales price - (Sales price X discount (%))

Discounted price = 1000 - (1000 X 15(%))

Discounted price = **850**

Scenario #2

In the same Bookshop, Manny's nephew came and bought the same book worth 1000 Php. Since the Customer is his nephew and a family member, He gave an additional 5%.

Answer:

Formula:

1st Discounted price = primary sales price - (sales price X 1st discount (%))

1st Discounted price = 1000 - (1000 X 15(%))

1st Discounted price = 850

Then

2nd Discounted price = 1st discounted price- (1st discount price X 2nd discount (%))

2nd Discounted price = 850 – (850 x 5%)

2nd Discounted price = **807.50**

Note: remember that a 15% then 5% discount is different from a 15% discount.

A 15% then 5% discount on the sales price of 1000 can yield 807.50 Php

While a 15% discount will yield 850 Php hence a 15% plus 5% will give buyers better advantage. The steps and formula are fairly straight forward hence you just have to follow the steps.

Cash Discounts

Cash discounts are reductions granted by the seller of goods and service in order to motivate buyers to pay within a specific time or period. Sellers usually record cash discounts as sales discounts and buyers usually record this as purchase discounts. They usually noted in fraction form.

Example :

$$\frac{2}{5} = \frac{n}{15}$$

Question: What does this mean in terms of Cash discount $\frac{2}{5}$ $= \frac{n}{15}$?

Answer:

$\frac{2}{5}$ (2 % discount if paid within 5 days)

$\frac{n}{15}$ (After 5 day, buyer has to pay the regular price within 15 days or else penalties will be imposed in form of additional interest)

Scenario #1

Alvin owns an appliance center. As a reward to his loyal customers, he offers a cash discount of $\frac{2}{5} = \frac{1}{10} = \frac{n}{20}$. One his loyal customer bought a TV worth 100,000 Php on exactly march 1?

Question# 1. How much is the cash discount based on the schedule given?

Answer:

$\frac{2}{5}$ means 2% discount if payment was made from march 1 to 5

Formula: Discounted price = 100,000 - (100,000 X 2%)

Discounted price = 98,000 if paid within 5 days

$\frac{1}{10}$ means 1% discount if payment was made from march 6 to 10

Formula: Discounted price = 100,000 - (100,000 X 1%)

Discounted price = <u>99,000 if paid within March 6th -</u>

<u>10th days</u>

$\frac{n}{15}$ means no discount if payment was made from

march 11 to 15

Formula: Discounted price = 100,000 - (100,000 X 0%)

Discounted price = <u>100,000 if paid within March 11th</u>

<u>-15th</u>

If paid later than Dec 15 penalties will be applicable

thru interest.

Scenario #2

Alvin owns an appliance center. His sister bought a TV worth

100,000 Php on exactly march 1? He gave her trade discount

of 10% and 3 % and offer a cash discount of $\frac{2}{5} = \frac{1}{10} = \frac{n}{20}$.

Question# 1. How do you compute for the discounted price after trade discount?

Answer:

Formula:

1st Discounted price = primary sales price - (sales price X 1st discount (%))

1st Discounted price = 100,000 - (100,000 X 10%)

1st Discounted price = 90,000

Then

2nd Discounted price = 1st discounted price- (1st discount price X 2nd discount (%))

2nd Discounted price = 90,000 – (90,000 x 3%)

2nd Discounted price = **87,300**

How much is the cash discount based on the schedule given?

$\frac{2}{5}$ means 2% discount if payment was made from march 1 to 5

Formula: Discounted price = 87,300 - (87,300 X 2%)

Discounted price = <u>85,554 if paid within 5 days</u>

$\frac{1}{10}$ means 1% discount if payment was made from march 6 to 10

Formula: Discounted price = 87,300 - (87,300 X 1%)

Discounted price = <u>86,427 if paid within March 6th -</u>
<u>10th days</u>

$\frac{n}{15}$ means no discount if payment was made from march 11 to 15

Formula: Discounted price = 87,300 - (87,300 X 0%)

Discounted price = <u>87,300 if paid within March 11th -</u>
<u>15th</u>

If paid later than Dec 15 penalties will be applicable thru interest.

Post Chapter Activity #11

Topic: Discount

Question 1

Eric wants to buy a vacuum cleaner worth 7,000 pesos with a 10% discount. How much is the new discounted price?

Question 2

Alvin wants to buy the same vacuum cleaner. He was given an additional 5% discount because his uncle is the manager of the shop. How much is his new discount price?

Question 3

Joan want to buy a car worth 300,000 from a car shop of her friend. She was given a cash discount of $\frac{5}{6} = \frac{3}{10} = \frac{n}{20}$. Explain the cash discount given to her.

Lesson 12:

Profit and Loss

Profits is a financial gain that is realized when the business' revenue exceeds company's expenses while **Loss** is a financial deficit that is realized when the company's expenses exceed business revenue.

Usually in a business math our focus has to be geared toward the scale of Micro Small and Medium Enterprise hence we will focus on profit and loss in selling a business product or service. This can be explained better thru the use break-even ratio but before we do this. Let us first go thru an Income statement which is also called Profit and Loss statement.

➢ **INCOME STATEMENT**

It is a financial statement that presents a company's financial performance over a specific accounting period of time. It will show the company's revenue and cost which vital for us to access the financial strength of the company. It is also called *Profit and Loss statement* or *revenue and expense statements*.

Some of the items included in the income statement are the following:

1. ***Gross Annual Sales***. It is the total revenue or sale that your company have accumulated in a year

2. ***Cost of Goods sale***. These are the direct costs that are attributed to the production of your product and service. (Raw materials, Direct Labor cost, and etc.)

3. ***Gross Profit***. the difference between Gross Annual Sales and Cost of Goods sales

4. ***Selling, General and Administrative Cost***. These are the cost that incurs which are not directly attributed to the manufacturing of product and service. (selling expense, promoting expense, distribution cost, rent, utilities, mortgage, wages, administrative expense, warranties, insurances, and etc)

5. **Operating Income**. The difference between Gross Profit and Selling, General and Administrative Cost. This an income incur from the operation of the company.

6. **Net income**. The difference between the Operation income and Taxes.

Example# Income Statement		
Marie's Flower Shop		
Income statement		
For the Year ending Dec. 31, 2016		
Gross Annual Sales	800,000	
Less:		
Cost of Goods Sold		
Seeds	50,000	
Fertilizer	20,000	
Labor	200,000	
Mineralized Water	10,000	
Gross Profit		520,000
Less:		
SGA	60,000	

Rent	100,000	
Salary	50,000	
Insurance	30,000	
Utilities	20,000	
promotional		
Operating income		260,000
Less:	30,000	
Taxes		
Net Profit:		230,000

> ➤ **Break-even point analysis**

It is the process used to determine the number of units (product / service) that your company has to sell to cover the whole operational cost of the business hence considering the sales break-even.

Formula:

Break-even point per unit (BEPU) = Fixed cost / (price per unit – variable cost)

Fixed cost are expense of the company that don't change over a relevant value of time (e.g. property, insurance, equipment, utilities and etc.) These are cost that don't change over production or are not affected by manufacturing cost.

Variable cost are expenses or cost of the company that are dependent on the number of units produced (e.g. raw material, assembly cost, direct labor, etc)

Sample of Break-even point per unit

Manuel's Shoe Factory

Break-Even Point Analysis

FIXED COST: 100,000 PHP

Variable Cost per Pair of shoe = 200 PHP

Cost of a Pair of Shoe = 1000 PHP

BEPU=FC/(PRICE per unit –VC)

BEPU = 100,000 / (1000-200)

BEPU = 125 Units

BEPP or Break-Even Point in Pesos = BEPU x PRICE per unit

BEPP = 125 units x1000

BEPP = 125,000 pesos

Conclusion: a sale of 125 units can make the company a break-even in profit.

Anything higher than 125 unit sold is positive income and anything lower than 125 unit sold is negative income.

If you think 125 unit is impossible to sell and that selling 100 units is more feasible, you have some optional variable adjustment to consider.

1. Reduce your fixed cost. (E.g. decrease your FC to 80,000)
2. Increase your price per unit (E.g. increase your PPU to 1200)
3. Reduce your VC in combination with other variable adjustments (E.g. Increase PPU by 1100 and reduce VC to 100)

Post Chapter Activity #12

Topic: Profit and Loss

1. Calculate for the Break-even point analysis of the following scenario.

Scenario #1 Mathew has a leather bag manufacturing company	
Insurance cost	1,000.00 Php/month
Rental Cost	10,000 Php/month
utilities	2,000.00 Php/month
Raw materials	500.00 Php/ bag
assembly cost	200.00 Php/bag
Price of leather bag	1,500.00 Php/bag

How many leather bags does Mathew's company have to produce to be considered Break-even on sales? (Write your computation below.)

If Mathew's company can only produce 15 bags per month, how much adjustment in the price can he make to be considered break-even on sale? (Write your computation below.)

Interest

Interest in business refers to the cost of borrowing money. Usually, interest is applicable to borrowing money from either formal or informal lenders. In business, borrowing money is an important part of doing business particularly for business operation and expansion hence understanding how interest work should be a critical part of financial education.

The two type of interest are **simple interest** and **compounding interest**.

1. **Simple interest** is a quick and easy way to compute interest on a borrowed money or loan. It is most commonly used in business. We will focus on this type of interest rate.

   Formula: I = PRT

   I= interest
   P= principal amount
   R=rate in decimal
   T= time in years

If you want to compute for the total **Future Value**

Formula: F = P + I

F= future value
P= principle amount
I = interest

Example of simple interest

Scenario 1: James needed a copying machine for his business. He borrowed 300,000 with a 6% annual interest which is payable 5 years from his cooperative lender. How much are the interest and the future value?

Answer:
I = PRT
I = 300,000 x 0.05 x 5
I = **75,000**
Simple interest is 75,000

F = P + I
F= 300,000 + 75,000
F= **375,000**

Scenario 2. Alvin invested in a savings bank that earns 2% per year with simple interest. He deposited 100,000 for 4 years. How much will he earn?

Answer:
I = PRT

I = 100,000 x 0.02 x 4
I = **8,000**

Scenario 3. Mario wants to borrow 7,000 at 5% interest rate. He is willing to pay 1,050 for interest. How many years does he have to pay his loan?

Answer:
Time = FV / Payments
T = (7,000 x 105%) / 1,050
T = 7,350 / 1,050
T = 7
He has **7 months**

If you want to incorporate Future Value of Simple interest formula into your Microsoft Excel, you can use the following formula and pattern. =H4*(1+H5*H6)

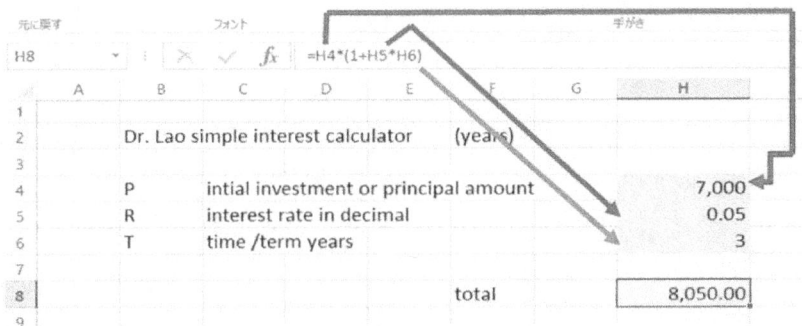

2. **Compound interest**: Similarly to simple interest, your principle will earn interest. Unlike a simple interest, the interest is not fixed but is reinvested together with the principle to earn a bigger interest. This is commonly used by credit card companies and other investment vehicles to earn bigger interest. It will earn more than a simple interest.

The basic principle of compound interest is earning

additional interest on interest.

Once you earn your **first** interest payment, it is **added** to the principle.

| 1000 + 9% | 1090 + 9% | 1188.10 + 9% | 1295.03 + 9% |
| Year 1 | Year 2 | Year 3 | Year 4 |

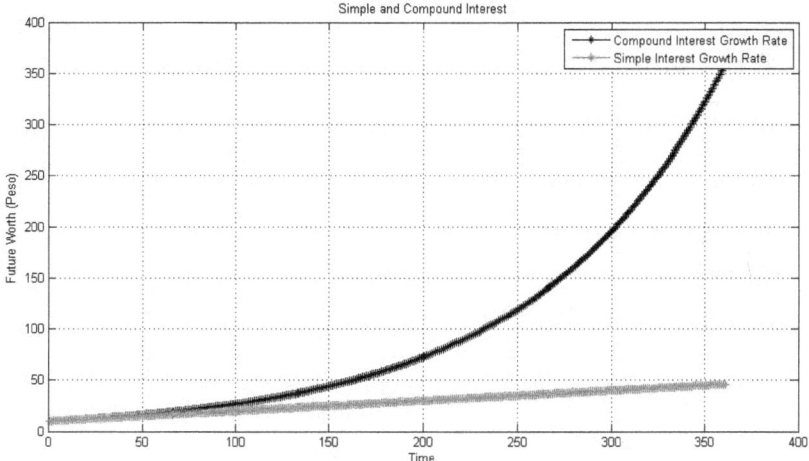

Formula:

Amount

$$A = P\left(1 + \frac{r}{n}\right)^{nt}$$

Principal — rate of interest — time in years — number of times per year, interest is compounded

Example of compounding interest

Scenario 1:
Michael was offered by his bank a Bond investment that can yield 4% compounding interest monthly with a holding time of 5 years. He invested 200,000. How much will he get after the holding time?

Formula:
A = P (1 + r/n) ^nt
A = 200,000 (1 + 0.04/12)^12(5)
A = 244,199.32

If we compared use these parameters in a Simple discount. Let us compare.

I = PRT
I = 200,000 x 0.04 x 5
I = **40,000**
Simple interest is 40,000

F = P + I
F= 200,000 + 40,000
F= **240,000**

Hence we can see that compounding interest yields greater than a simple discount.

Scenario 2:

Michael was offered by his bank a Bond investment that can yield 4% compounding interest monthly with a holding time of 5 years. He invested 200,000. **He decided to put an additional 5,000.00 monthly invested at the end of every month**. How much will he get after the holding time? (PMT = monthly payment)

Answer:

Total Amount = (A compound interest) + (FV series with monthly deposit)
A = P (1 + r/n) ^nt
FV = PMT x ((1 + r/n)^nt – 1) / (r/n))

Formula:
$A = P (1 + r/n)^{nt}$
$A = 200{,}000 (1 + 0.04/12)^{12(5)}$
A = 244,199.32

$FV = PMT \times ((1 + r/n)^{nt} - 1) / (r/n))$
$FV = 5{,}000 \times ((1 + 0.04/12)^{12(5)} - 1) / (0.04/12))$
$FV = 5{,}000 \times ((1 + 0.0033)^{60} - 1) / (0.0033))$
$FV = 5{,}000 \times ((1.0033)^{60} - 1) / (0.0033))$
$FV = 5{,}000 \times ((1.219 - 1) / (0.0033))$
$FV = 5{,}000 \times ((0.219) / (0.0033))$
$FV = 5{,}000 \times ((0.219) / (0.0033))$
$FV = 5{,}000 \times 66.36$
FV = 331,800

Total amount = A + FV
Total amount = 244,199.32 + 331,800
Total amount = 575,999.32

This is nice to know and the difficulty to compute. It is harder and longer than usual. This may vary due to rounding of decimal places and other factors. I will make it easier for you by my excel instruction. My goal is to make things easier for you.

This is the Microsoft Excel Formula for compounding interest: =H3*(1+H4/H6)^(H5*H6)

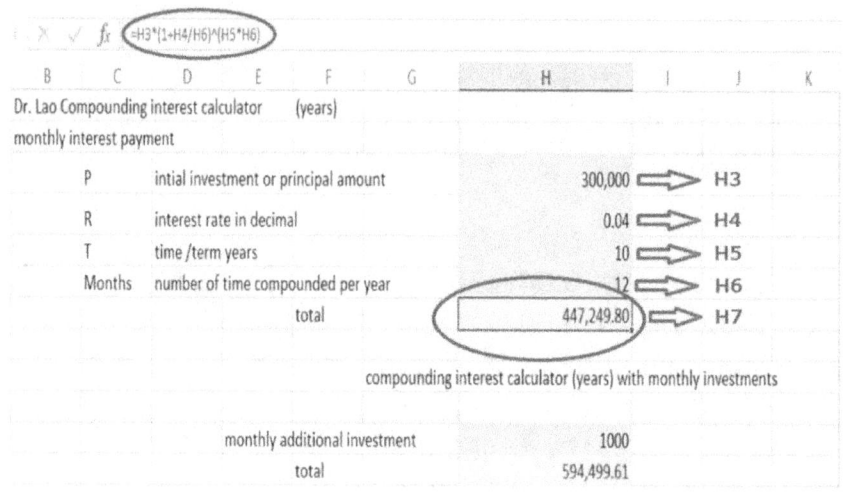

This is the Microsoft Excel Formula for compounding interest with additional monthly deposits at the end of each month:
=FV(H4/H6,H5*H6,-H11,-H3)

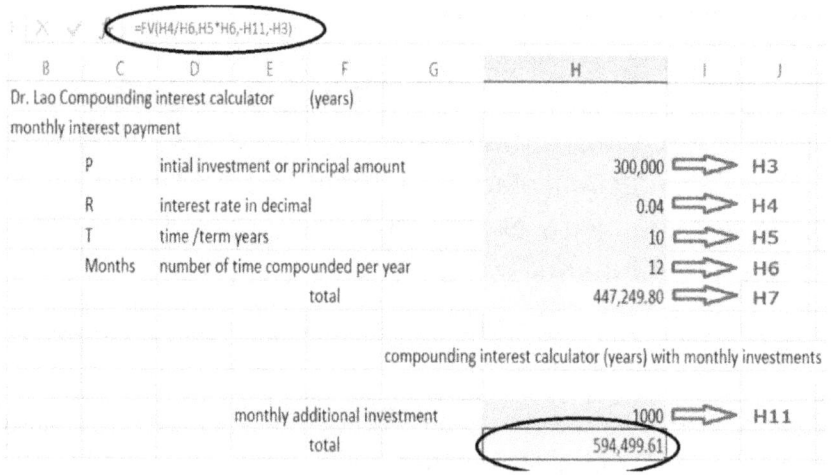

Summary:

1. If you are going to choose an investment, Compound interest investment with monthly additional payment will yield best results compared to simple interest.
2. In choosing a loan, simple and fixed interest is preferred.
3. In using a credit card, always pay the full amount every end of the billing month. If you pay the minimum payment, your unpaid balance will compound monthly hence some people will end up in huge credit card Debt.

Post Chapter Activity #13

Topic: Interest

Question 1

You want to start deposit your 500,000 in a bank with a fixed interest rate of 3% per year. If you put your money there for 5 years, how much will your money earn?

Question 2

Alvin invested his money worth 100,000 to buy corporate bonds with a 5% compounding interest and holding period of 5 years. He plans to add 2,000 pesos per month on his investment for 5 years. How much will be his total investment after holding period ends?

Loan

A <u>Loan</u> in business terms is an act of giving money, property, supply or service, in exchange for future full repayment of the amount plus interest or other financial charges. There are two characters in a loan. They are the Lender and Lendee.

The **Lender** is the one who lends the money, service, property or supply. They can be consist of one person, a group of people or a financial institution.

The **Lendee** is the one who borrows money, service, property or supply from the Lender.

Before the Lender and Lendee agrees on a loan they must decide on the term of the loan

The terms of a loan includes the purpose of the loan, length of the payment term, amount of the loan, collateral, down payment, and etc.

The lender will assess the lender's ability to pay hence lender will look at the Lendee's financial history.

Examples of some types of loans:

1. Student Loan – a loan offered to college students to pay for their education
2. Mortgage – a loan offered for the purpose of purchasing a house.
3. Auto loan - a loan offered for the purpose of purchasing a car.
4. Personal Loan – a loan offered to preferred clients for the purchased of personal item.
5. Small business Loan– a loan offered to entrepreneur for business purpose
6. Payday Loan– a loan offered to employees to bridge a gap from one paycheck to the other. It is usually used for living expenses.

Amortization is a term used to refer to the process of scheduled payments of loan balance with interest. The length of time for amortization will depend on the agreement between the lender and lendee.

Formula for monthly payment

$A = ((i \times P \times (1+i)^n) / ((1+i)^n - 1)$

A = monthly payments

I = monthly interest rate = annual interest/12

P = loan's initial amount

N = total number of payments in months

Example for Amortization computation

Scenario 1. Andrew loaned 100,000.00 from the bank as a business loan. His amortization payment term is 5 years at a fix rate of 5%. How much is the monthly Payments?

$A = ((i \times P \times (1+i)^n) / ((1+i)^n - 1)$
$A = ((\ 0.00417 \ \times \ 100,000 \ \times \ (1+0.00417)^{60} \ ) \ / \ ((1+0.00417)^{60} - 1)$
A = **1890.49 / month** for 60 months

This is nice to know and the difficulty to compute. This may vary due to rounding of decimal places, calculator used and other factors. I will make it easier for you by using my excel instruction. My goal is to make things easier for you.

Instruction on how to build an amortization schedule of payment for excel:

Step 1 build up the excel structure. Insert the formula in cell B5 "=PMT(B4/12,B3*B2,-B1)"

		fx	=PMT(B4/12,B3*B2,-B1)		

A	B	C	D	E	F
Loan amount	PHP 100,000.00			sum of interest	PHP 13,227.40
loan term (years)	5				
payment per year	12				
annual interest rate	5%				
one time payment	PHP 1,887.12				

Period	Beginning balance	Payment	Principal	Interest	Ending balance
1	PHP 100,000.00	PHP 1,887.12	PHP 1,470.46	416.67	PHP 98,529.54
2	PHP 98,529.54	PHP 1,887.12	PHP 1,476.58	410.54	PHP 97,052.96
3	PHP 97,052.96	PHP 1,887.12	PHP 1,482.74	404.39	PHP 95,570.22
4	PHP 95,570.22	PHP 1,887.12	PHP 1,488.91	398.21	PHP 94,081.31
5	PHP 94,081.31	PHP 1,887.12	PHP 1,495.12	392.01	PHP 92,586.19
6	PHP 92,586.19	PHP 1,887.12	PHP 1,501.35	385.78	PHP 91,084.84
7	PHP 91,084.84	PHP 1,887.12	PHP 1,507.60	379.52	PHP 89,577.24
8	PHP 89,577.24	PHP 1,887.12	PHP 1,513.88	373.24	PHP 88,063.36
9	PHP 88,063.36	PHP 1,887.12	PHP 1,520.19	366.93	PHP 86,543.16

Step 2 insert the formula in "=B1" B8

Step 3 insert the formula "=$B$5" in C8

Step 4. Insert the formula "=PPMT($B$4/12,A8,$B$2*$B$3,-$B$1)" in D8

Step 5. Insert the formula "=IPMT($B$4/12,A8,$B$2*$B$3,-$B$1)" in E8

Step 6. Insert the formula "=B8-D8" in F8

Step 7. Insert the formula "=F8" in B9

Step 8. Insert the formula "=$B$5" in C9

Step 9. Insert the Formula "=PPMT($B$4/12,A9,$B$2*$B$3,-$B$1)" in D9

Step 10. Insert the Formula "=IPMT($B$4/12,A9,$B$2*$B$3,-$B$1)" in E9 and "=B9-D9" in F9

Step 11. Insert the Formula "=F9" in B10

Step 12. Insert the Formula "=SUM(E8:E67)" in F1

Step 13. Select the cell B8 to B10 and drag it down

Step 14. Select the cell C8 to C9 and drag it down

Step 15. Select the cell D8 to D9 and drag it down

Step 16. Select the cell E8 to E9 and drag it down

Step 17. Select the cell D8 to D9 and drag it down

	B8	▾ : ✕ ✓ *fx*	=B1			

	A	B	C	D	E	F
1	Loan amount	PHP 100,000.00			sum of interest	PHP 13,227.40
2	loan term (years)	5				
3	payment per year	12				
4	annual interest rate	5%				
5	one time payment	PHP 1,887.12				
6						
7	Period	Beginning balance	Payment	Principal	Interest	Ending balance
8	1	PHP 100,000.00	PHP 1,887.12	PHP 1,470.46	416.67	PHP 98,529.54
9	2	PHP 98,529.54	PHP 1,887.12	PHP 1,476.58	410.54	PHP 97,052.96
10	3	PHP 97,052.96	PHP 1,887.12	PHP 1,482.74	404.39	PHP 95,570.22
11	4	PHP 95,570.22	PHP 1,887.12	PHP 1,488.91	398.21	PHP 94,081.31
12	5	PHP 94,081.31	PHP 1,887.12	PHP 1,495.12	392.01	PHP 92,586.19
13	6	PHP 92,586.19	PHP 1,887.12	PHP 1,501.35	385.78	PHP 91,084.84
14	7	PHP 91,084.84	PHP 1,887.12	PHP 1,507.60	379.52	PHP 89,577.24
15	8	PHP 89,577.24	PHP 1,887.12	PHP 1,513.88	373.24	PHP 88,063.36

As you can see, we will pay a fixed amount of PHP 1,887.12 every month. We can also notice that the interest payment go down while the principal payment goes up as we proceed thru the months.

Post Chapter Activity #14

Topic: Loan

Question 1

Ace loaned 100,000 from his cooperative bank for medical expenses. With a term of 1 year to pay and 5% fixed interest, write down his amortization schedule and monthly payments starting from month 1 to month 12.

Lesson 15:

Commission and overrides

A commission is a service charge given by a company to the agent, salesman, investment advisor or an individual who help in facilitating a sale.

Overrides are commissions given to managers of sales agents that facilitated or secured a sale.

There are two basic types of commission:

a. Plain commission- it is a situation when a sales agent is not given any salary but her compensation is fully based on sales commission. People with plain commissions are more driven and motivated to achieve a sale otherwise they will be empty handed.

b. Commission plus salary – it is a situation when sales agent is given Basic salary in addition to the sales commission.

Table 15.1 Examples of plain commission, commission plus salary, and overrides

Scenario #1
Anita is working part-time for an appliance company. She is working on Plain commission. The company is giving her 8% commission on all appliance that she sells. Last month she sold a total of Php 200,000 worth of appliance. How much is her commission? Answer: In this situation, we will use the P=BR formula P= Php 200,000 x 8% P= Php 16,000   Scenario # 2 Anita was hired full-time by the same appliance company because of her outstanding sales record. She is now working with a basic salary of Php 10,000 and a sales commission of 5%. That same she sold Php 200,000 worth of appliance. How much are her gross earnings? Answer: Gross earnings = basic salary + commission Gross earnings = Php 10,000 + (Php 200,000 x 5%) Gross earnings = Php 10,000 + Php 10,000 Gross earnings = Php 20,000

Scenario # 3

Anita did a splendid Job. She has a natural skill for sales. The company promoted her to store manager. She was given 3 salespeople working under her. The company increased her basic pay to Php 13,000. Her sales commission was still at 5% plus she will get 1% of the total sale of the 3 sales people working under her. If she sold Php 200,000 worth of appliances and the total sales of the 3 sales people under her was worth 500,000, How much is her gross earnings?

Answer:
Gross earnings = basic salary + commission + overrides
Gross earnings = 13,000 + (200,000 x 5%) + (500,000 x 1%)
Gross earnings = 13,000 + 10,000 + 5,000
Gross earnings = Php 28,000

Scenario # 4

James is working for a travel agent. His basic salary is 15,000. He is also given 3% on sale that exceeds 100,000. This month his sale reached up to 130,000. How much is his gross earnings?

Answer:
Gross earnings = basic salary + commission
Gross earnings = 15,000 + [(130,000 - 100,000) x 3%]
Gross earnings = 15,000 + [30,000 x 3%]
Gross earnings = 15,000 + 900
Gross Earnings = 15,900

Post Chapter Activity #15

Topic: Commission and Overrides

Question 1

Maria is a soap sales woman. She earns thru plain commission of 10% of monthly sale only. Last month, she sold 500,000 pesos worth of soap. How much will be her take home pay?

Question 2

Melvin is a tooth paste sales man with a basic salary of 10,000 pesos and a 3 % sales commission. He sold 100,000 pesos worth of tooth paste that month. How much is his take home pay for the month?

Question 3

Martin is a book salesman. He has a basic pay of 15,000 pesos a month with a direct sales commission of 3%. He has 5 people working for him and he will be given a commission of 1% for their respective sale. Last month he sold a total of 70,000 pesos and his team sold a total of 300,000 pesos. How much is his take home pay ?

Lesson 16:

Wages, Salary, and benefits

Wages are defined as hourly compensation for work. Often times they are called hourly employees. They work a maximum of 8 hours and are given overtime pay if asked to work longer. Usually, wages are applied to blue collar jobs.

Salary are workers paid monthly or semi-monthly. Their contribution to the company cannot be easily measured by hourly rate. Salary are usually applied to white collar job.

Table 16.1 Current Daily Minimum Wage Rate (NCR effective: 05 October 2017)

Sector	Basic wage	Basic wage increase	New Basic wage	COLA	New Minimum wage increase
Non agriculture	481.00	21.00	502.00	10.00	512.00
Agriculture (plantation and non-plantation)	444.00	21.00	465.00	10.00	475.00
Retail/service	444.00	21.00	465.00	10.00	475.00

establishment employing 15 people or less					
Manufacturing Establishment regularly employed less than 10	444.00	21.00	465.00	10.00	475.00

(Source https://www.nwpc.dole.gov.ph/pages/ncr/cmwr.html)

Remember that working for more than 8 hours, employees are entitled for over overtime pay.

Over time pay is computed as <u>overtime pay</u> = number of hours that exceeds 8 hours x 25%

Table 16.2 example of overtime pay computation

Example: Maria is a master welder and getting paid 1000 / day. Today she worked for 10 hours. Compute for her overtime pay and total pay for the day. Answer: Daily pay is 1000/day Hourly pay: 1000/8 = 125.00/ hour

Overtime hours: 10 hours – 8 hours = 2 hours

Overtime pay = 2 x [125 +(125 x25%)] = 312.50
or
Overtime pay = 2 x [125 x125%] = 312.50

Total pay for the day: daily rate + overtime pay = 1000 x 312.50 = **1,312.50**

In some instances, we are asked by our employer to work on our rest day, regular holiday or special holiday. The next table will make it easier imagine and compute for our compensation.

Table 16.3 comparison between regular holiday and special holiday

Regular holiday (2017)	Special Non-working holiday (2017)
New years	Chinese new year
Araw ng Kagitingan	Edsa Revolution
Maundy Thursday	Black Saturday
Good Friday	Ninoy Aquino day
Labor day	Last day of the year
Independence day	
Eid'l Fitr	
National heroes day	
Eidul Adha	
Bonifacio day	
Christmas day	

Rizal day	

Table 16.4 comparison between rest day, regular holiday and special holiday payments for work.

- On a rest day **or** special holiday, the Hourly rate = 130% x regular hourly rate

For example, Janice is working as a sales lady with a minimum wage of 512 / day or 64/hour. Her boss asks her to work on her rest day. How much will she get for 8 hours of work?

Hourly rate for rest day = 64 x 130% = 83.2

Days wage on a rest day = hourly rate for rest day x 8 = 83.2 x 8 = 665.60 pesos

What if she has 2 hours of overtime?
Over time pay on rest day= hourly rate for rest day x 2 x 130%
Over time pay on rest day= 83.2 x 2 x 130% = 216.32

Gross pay for the whole rest day = 881.92

- On a rest day **of** special holiday, the Hourly rate on a rest day = 150% x regular hourly rate

For example, Janice is working as a sales lady with a minimum wage of 512 / day or 64/hour. Her boss asks her to work on her rest day <u>which fall on a special holiday</u>. How much will she get for 8 hours of work?

Hourly rate for a rest day on a special holiday = Hourly rate x 150%

Hourly rate for a rest day on a special holiday = 64x 150%

= <u>96</u>

Days wage on a rest day which falls on a special holiday = 96 x 8 = <u>768</u>

What if she has 2 hours of overtime?

Over time pay on rest day of a special holiday= hourly rate for rest day of a special holiday x 2 x 130%

Over time pay on rest day of a special holiday= 96 x 2 x 130% = <u>249.60</u>

Gross pay for the whole rest day = <u>1,017.60</u>

- <u>On a regular holiday</u>, the Hourly rate on a regular holiday= 200% x regular hourly rate

For example, Janice is working as a sales lady with a minimum wage of 512 / day or 64/hour. Her boss asks her to work on a <u>regular holiday</u>. How much will she get for 8 hours of work?

Hourly rate on a regular holiday= 200% x regular hourly rate = 200% x 64 = 128/ hour

Days wage on regular holiday = 128 x 8 = <u>1024</u>

- <u>On a regular holiday</u>, the Hourly rate on a regular holiday= 200% x regular hourly rate

For example, Janice is working as a sales lady with a minimum wage of 512 / day or 64/hour. Her boss asks her to work on a <u>regular holiday</u>. How much will she get for 8 hours of work?

Hourly rate on a regular holiday= 200% x regular hourly rate = 200% x 64 = 128/ hour

Days wage on regular holiday = 128 x 8 = <u>1024</u>

What if she have 2 hours of overtime?

Over time pay on regular holiday= hourly rate on regular

holiday x 2 x 130%

Over time pay on regular holiday= 128 x 2 x 130% =<u>332.80</u>

Gross pay for the whole rest day = 1024 + 332.80 = 1,356.80

- On a rest day **of** regular holiday, the Hourly rate on a rest day = 260% x regular hourly rate

For example, Janice is working as a sales lady with a minimum wage of 512 / day or 64/hour. Her boss asks her to work on her rest day which fall on a regular holiday. How much will she get for 8 hours of work?

Hourly rate on a rest day of regular holiday= 260% x regular hourly rate = 260% x 64 = 166.40/ hour

Days wage on rest day of regular holiday = 166.40 x 8 = 1,331.20

What if she has 2 hours of overtime?

Over time pay on rest day of regular holiday= hourly rate on rest day of regular holiday x 2 x 130%

Over time pay on rest day of regular holiday= 166.40 x 2 x 130% = 432.64

Gross pay for the whole rest day = 1,331.20 + 432.64 = 1,763.84

Basic Benefit of employees in the Philippines:

13th month pay is mandatory under the presidential decree No. 851. It says all employee that worked for at least 1 month , regardless of their work status, are entitled to a 13th month pay.

Retirement pay is a payment made to employees that reach 60 years old and who had rendered at least 5 years of work in the company. It is computed at ½ of the latest monthly salary for ever year of service. (The ½ month salary includes: 1/12 of 13th month pay, cash equivalent of 5 days of service incentive leave, and 15 days salary based on the latest salary rate.)

Night shift differential – applies to employees who work during 10 pm to 6 am. An additional 10% is applied on their hours of service

Leave benefits – it is common practice to give employees benefit leave like sick leave, vacation leave or emergency leave as the need arise. There is also mandatory leave like maternity leave, paternity leave, parental leave for solo parents, and special leave for woman.

SSS contribution – this contribution is equivalent to 11% of monthly salary but doesn't exceed 16,000.00. It is shared by the employee (3.63%) and employer (7.37%). The table for SSS contribution can be seen on the SSS website. Its government counterpart is the GSIS

Philhealth contribution - this benefit is important for employees and employee's dependents in cases of occurrence of sickness. It is shared by the employee and employer 50/50 based on the salary bracket. The table for Philhealth salary bracket can be seen on the Philhealth website.

PAGIBIG Fund Contribution – the Home development mutual fund that is shared by employees and employers. It ranges from 1-2 % of the employee's salary. The fund can be used for housing loans, multipurpose loans, and etc.

INCOME TAX

Income tax is the tax imposed on individuals or entities on their respective earned income derived from either wages, commission or salaries.

For a while, Filipino employee's income tax was based on the 1997 Philippine tax code, but on Dec 19, 2017, President Rodrigo Duterte signed into law R.A. 10963 or the Tax Reform for Acceleration and Inclusion (TRAIN) bill. This bill was meant to shift the tax burden from the low and middle wage earners to the wealthiest in the community.

Table 16.5 comparison between 1997 tax code vs the TRAIN

1997 TAX CODE	TRAIN LAW

ANNUAL TAXABLE INCOME	TAX RATE	ANNUAL TAXABLE INCOME (2018-2022)	TAX RATE
Not over than 10,000	5%	Not over than 250,000	0%
Over 10,000 - 30,000	500Php +10% of the excess of 10,000	Over 250,000 - 400,000	20% of the excess of 250,000
Over 30,000-70,000	2,500Php +15% of the excess of 30,000	Over 400,000-800,000	30,000Php +25% of the excess of 400,000
Over 70,000-140,000	8,500Php +20% of the excess of 70,000	Over 800,000-2,000,000	130,000Php +30% of the excess of 800,000
Over 140,000-250,000	22,500Php +25% of the excess of 140,000	Over 2,000,000-8,000,000	490,000Php +32% of the excess of 2,000,000
Over 250,000 – 500,000	50,000Php +30% of the excess of 250,000	Over 8,000,000	2,410,000Php +35% of the excess of 8,000,000
Over 500,000	125,000Php +32% of the excess of 500,000		

Post Chapter Activity #16

Topic: Commission and Overrides

Question 1

Sheila is a hairdresser for Inday's beauty parlor. Her daily wage is 700/day.

1. Her boss asked her to work for 12 hours. How much is her pay for the day?

2. What if her boss asked her to work for 8 hours on her rest day?

3. What if her boss asked her to work for 8 hours on her rest day which falls on a special holiday?

4. What if her boss asked her to work for 8 hours on a regular holiday?

5. What if her boss asked her to work for 8 hours on her rest day which falls on a regular holiday?

Lesson 17.

Business Data

Business Data are information like the business rule, people, events or things that can be utilized in business operations and analysis. For the purpose of this book, we will make it as simple, comprehensible and applicable as possible.

Most business data are usually presented either textual, tabular or graphical for easy comprehension hence we will break-it out to different parts. Textual, tabular and graphical data presentation.

1. Textual Presentation Data – are data that are presented in written in sentence, phrase or paragraph form. This type of data presentation is more comprehensive and descriptive in nature.

   Example:
   ABC restaurant had 500 customers last month. Customers were 200 or 40 % male and 300 or 60% female. 50 or 5% are the senior citizens. 369 or 73.8% ordered Spring Chicken while 131 or 26.2% ordered sweet and sour fish.

2. Tabular Presentation of Data - Data are presented in tables were rows (horizontal) and column (vertical) are compared. It gives us a process to organized data and a capacity further statistically analyze data.

ABC restaurant customer profile vs Food orders

	Spring Chicken	Fried rice	Total
Male	100	100	200
Female	269	31	300
Total	369	131	500

3. Graphical presentation of data – data is presented visually thru charts or graphs. It is an effective way to present data in a more concise and understandable manner. The different graphic presentation styles are direct on the audience and based on the type of data to be presented. We will break-it down to 3 basic and most common types. Bar graph, Line Graph, and Pie graph.

a. Bar graph. They are data presented in rectangular bars. The Length of the bar corresponds to the quantity or the percentage of the category.

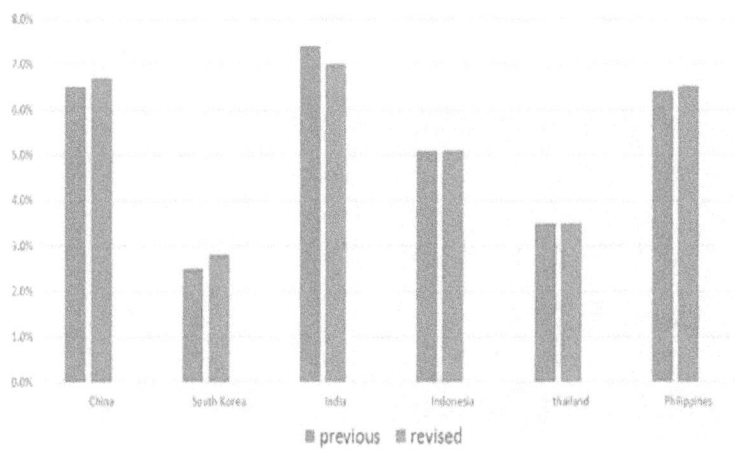

ADB Revised Asian 2017 GDP Forecast

(sources:
https://smartmoneypinoy.wixsite.com/main/single-post/2017/09/27/ADB-raises-2017-Developing-Asia%E2%80%99s-GDP-forecast)

b. Line graph – they are graphs that uses a line to connect data point to show changes in data over time and to demonstrate trends.

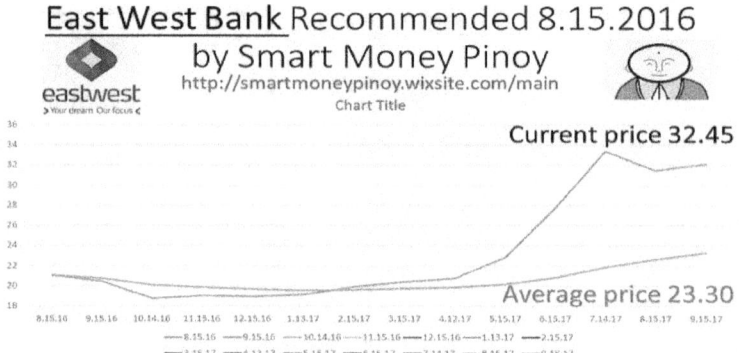

East West Bank Recommended 8.15.2016
by Smart Money Pinoy
http://smartmoneypinoy.wixsite.com/main
Chart Title

Current price 32.45

Average price 23.30

Earning of Php 9.15 per share 39.27% gain in 14 months

(sources:

https://smartmoneypinoy.wixsite.com/main/single-post/2017/10/03/East-West-Bank-gains-3927)

c. Pie Graph – are charts that demonstrate the visual proportions of the different part of data in relation to a whole data set. It can also be known as a circular chart.

Example of a chart graph.

Families in the Philippines by Floor Area of Housing Unit they Occupy

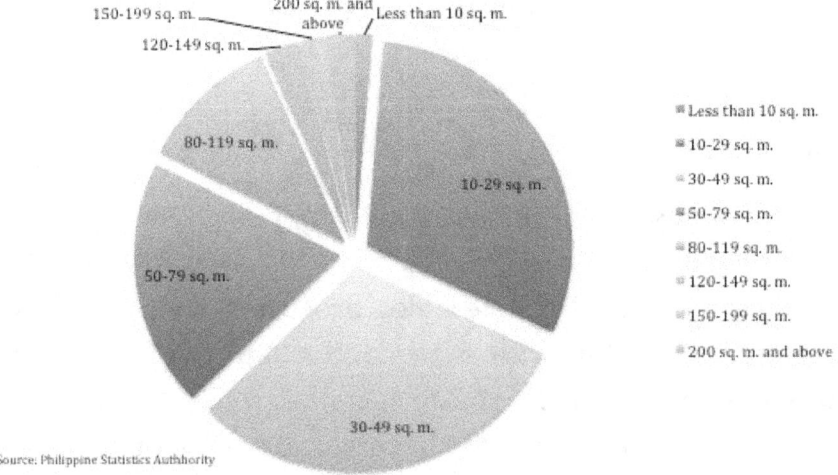

Source: Philippine Statistics Authhority

Legend:
- Less than 10 sq. m.
- 10-29 sq. m.
- 30-49 sq. m.
- 50-79 sq. m.
- 80-119 sq. m.
- 120-149 sq. m.
- 150-199 sq. m.
- 200 sq. m. and above

Post Chapter Activity #17

Topic: Business Data

Question 1

Company ABC telecom has 1000 subscribers. Demographics of his customer are 550 males and 450 females, 200 of the males and 100 of the females are using cellphone only service, while 350 of the males and 350 of the females are using cellphone with internet service. Make a table with Gender in Y axis while type of service on the X axis.

Question 2

Company ABC , XYZ and DEF are competitors in the telecom field. The 2016 gross profit of ABC is 50 million, XYZ is 30 million and DEF is 70 million. The 2017 gross profit of ABC is 30 million, XYZ is 50 million and DEF is 60 million. Make a bar graph that demonstrate these data.

Question 3

ABC telecom company's monthly earnings are 3 million on January, 4 million on February, 2 million on March, 3 million on April, 6 million on May, 7 million on June, 3 million on July, 2 million on August, 3 million on September, 2 million on October, 3 Million on November, and 5 million on December. Make a line graph demonstrating these data.

Question 4

DEF telecom's customer are located in 5 zones. Zone 1 has 20%, Zone 2 has 5%, Zone 3 has 30%, Zone 4 has 33%, and Zone 5 has 12% of the customers. Make a Pie Graph that can demonstrate these data.

Lesson 18.

Basic Business Data Analysis

Business data analysis is an important part in business operation particularly in the measurement of progress and survival. Its importance is not only limited to the business advancement but also to other beneficial endeavors such as to help in identify our clientele and resource allocations.

We will try to explain some basic statistic concepts the simplest way possible and on a superficial level. The deeper elaboration of the statistical concepts will discuss in a Statistic subject.

Measures of Central Tendency - It is often called center or location of distribution. It is a way of summarizing numerical data with a single number. It helps in simplifying a set of numbers hence its understanding will be helpful in business data analysis. The 3 most common measures of central tendency are arithmetic mean, median and mode.

  a. Mean are commonly referred to averages.
  b. Median is a number that divides a set of number into a middle
  c. Mode is the number that is most commonly occurring number in the set

---

Example: Ben sells ice-cream for a living. He recorded his sale for the year. Compute for the mean median and mode.

Table 18.1 Bens ice cream sales year 2017

Month	Number of ice-cream sold
1	10
2	7
3	7
4	9
5	12
6	13
7	15
8	8
9	4
10	6
11	5
12	4
Total	n = 100 (this is the total number of sales)

Mean = 100 (the total number of sales) / 12 (the number of months) = 8.33

      = 8.33 is the average sales of ice cream per month.

Mode = the number most commonly found in the set

      = 4 and 7

Median = (manual method) arrange the set numbers in order staring from the least to greater number

4,4,5,6,7,**7,8**,9,10,12,13,15

Since this set is an even number set, the middle number of this series are 7 and 8 hence we need to get the average. (7+8)/2 = 7.5

Median = 7.5

The Measure of Variability measures the variability or how much different each number are from one another. It also refers to the dispersion or spread between each of the members of a set.

What are tools in the measure of variability?

Range = highest number – lowest number

Example: in the set Ben's ice cream

Month	Number of ice-cream sold
1	10
2	7
3	7
4	9
5	12
6	13
7	15
8	8
9	4
10	6
11	5
12	4
Total	n = 100 (this is the total number of sales)

Range = 15-4 = <u>11</u>

A <u>range</u> can also be used to measure consistency particularly in the comparing between 2 or more. Caution has to be taken in using the range particularly in the presence of outliers that can invalidate the results.

Example: Barangay Basketball League's player 3 points: Alvin versus Mario

	Alvin's 3 point shots made	Mario's 3 point shots made
Game 1	4	7
Game 2	8	8
Game 3	9	5
Game 4	11	8
Game 5	2	6
Total score	34	34
Mean	6.8	6.8
Median	(2,4,**8**,9,11) = 8	(5,6,**7**,8,8) = 7
Mode	No mode	8
Range	11-2 = **9**	8-5 =**2 (more consistent)**

Standard Deviation – describes the average "distance" a data is from the middle of the dataset.

	Alvin's 3 point shots made	Alvin's 3 point shot –	Mario's 3 point shots made	Mario's 3 point shot –

		mean then squared		mean then squared
Game 1	4	4-6.8= - 2.8^2= **7.84**	7	7-6.8= - 0.2^2= **0.04**
Game 2	8	8-6.8= 1.2^2= **1.44**	8	8-6.8= 1.2^2= **1.44**
Game 3	9	9-6.8= 2.2^2= **4.84**	5	5-6.8= - 1.8^2= **3.24**
Game 4	11	11-6.8= 4.2^2= **17.64**	8	8-6.8= 1.2^2= **1.44**
Game 5	2	2-6.8 = -4.8^2 = **23.04**	6	6-6.8 = -0.8^2 = **0.64**
Total	34	**54.80**	34	**6.8**
Mean	6.8		6.8	
Median	(2,4,**8**,9,11) = 8		(5,6,**7**,8,8) = 7	
Mode	No mode		8	
Range	11-2 = **9**		8-5 =**2** **(more consistent)**	
Standard deviation	**3.7**		**1.30**	

To get the standard deviation

Step 1. Find the mean

Step 2. Subtract each number with the mean then square it

138

Step 3. Add the result (in this sample Alvin got 54.8 while Mario got 6.8)

Step 4. Divided it with N or the total number of sample minus 1 (N=5 ; so divide it with 4 which N-1) 54.8 / 4 = **13.7 for Alvin** while 17.6/4 =**1.7 for Mario**

Step 5. Finally find the square root of your result =**3.7 for Alvin** while **1.30 for Mario**

Step 6. My conclusion would be that Mario's standard deviation is 1.30 hence less variation compared to Alvin. Mario seems to be more consistent.

Test for Significant Difference

It is often used in experimentation, wherein set from 2 different subjects or source are compared and to examine if there is a significant difference between the 2. This part of the book is more informative in nature rather than instructive. Our main purpose is more to inform that such method exists and a further elaboration on this topic will be discussed in your statistic class.

(My aim is to make your life easier hence we will be using one of online calculator in https://www.mathportal.org/calculators/statistics-calculator/t-test-calculator.php)

T-Test- It is a type of test that compares one viable between 2 groups. (Example: testing for significant difference between the sale of regular pizza and pizza with pineapple) It is useful for a continuous variable.

Z-Test- is similar to t-test but used when the standard deviations are known and the sample size is large. (>30)

Points to consider:

1. Paired vs unpaired t-test:

Paired T-test is a type of t-test that deals with inter-subject variability or just one subject.

Unpaired T-test is a type of t-test that deals with 2 different groups of subject.

2. Equal vs unequal variance

Equal variance is homogeneity of variance. It simply assumes that the variances are equal along the group. We should consider it if we have an equal number of data points or numbers at nearly the same. Otherwise, we should assume they are unequal variances.

3. 1 tailed vs 2 tailed t-test

Two-tailed t-test is non-directional meaning you are trying to compare if one group is different from the second group.

One-tailed t-test is used to compare if one group is bigger or smaller than the other group. If the question states less than (left side of the curve) or greater than (right side of the curve) always consider 1 tailed t-test.

4. Null Hypothesis vs alternative hypothesis

Null hypothesis usually reflects no significant difference between the two groups being compared while alternative hypothesis usually reflects that there is a significant difference between the groups being compared.

5. Type I error vs type II error

Type I error is committed when there is an incorrect rejection of a true null hypothesis.

Type II error is committed when there is an incorrect acceptance of a false null hypothesis.

6. Significant level

Remember that we can only reject a Null hypothesis if the P- value is less than a predetermined level or α. α (alpha) is called the significant level. The significant level reflects the probability of committing a Type I error. Usually, the Significant Level is set at 5% or 0.05, 1% or 0.01, and 10% or 0.1, hence if set at 5% that means our study has 5 % risk of committing Type I error.

7. When to use a T-Test vs Z-test?

Preferably, we use a T-test is the population is less than 30 and if the Standard deviation is unknown. If the population is greater than 30 and the standard deviation is known then we use Z test.

Example of T-test in a research.

A research was done for a restaurant to understand the effects of adding pineapple in there pizza. They assigned group 1 are Pizza with pineapple while Group 2 are Pizza without pineapple.

They gave a questionnaire on the satisfaction on taste, wherein 0 is the lowest and 70 is the highest. Using α of 0.05 with 10 respondents, let us determine if there is a significant difference between the two groups.

Null Hypothesis: there is no significant difference between group 1 and group 2
alternative Hypothesis: there is a significant difference between group 1 and group 2

Subject	Group 1	Group 2
1	45	34
2	38	22
3	52	15
4	48	27
5	25	37
6	39	41
7	51	24
8	46	19

9	55	26
10	46	36

Let now go to the Website and input the following details. (https://www.mathportal.org/calculators/statistics-calculator/t-test-calculator.php)

Two sample t-test

Use this calculator to test whether population means are significantly different from each other.
Enter the numbers separated by comma(,) , colon(:), semicolon(;) or blank space.

Enter Data for Group 1

45,38,52,48,25,39,51,46,55,46

Enter Data for Group 2

34,22,15,27,37,41,24,19,26,36

☐ Use data grit to input values

1. Group description: ⑦
   - ◉ Groups Have Equal Variance (default)
   - ○ Groups Have Unequal Variance

2. Number of tails: ⑦
   - ◉ Two Tailed Test (default)
   - ○ One Tailed Test

3. Significance Level: ⑦
   - ◉ 0.05 (default)
   - ○ 0.01
   - ○ 0.001

4. Choose a test ⑦
   - ○ Unpaired T Test (default)
   - ◉ Paired (Dependent) T Test

☑ Show me the solution without an explanation

Find t and p value		Generate Example

Then we should Press **Find t and P value** for the results.

Result

You entered the following data:

Group 1								Group 2							
45	38	52	48	25	39	51	46	34	22	15	27	37	41	24	19
55	46							26	36						

The means of Group 1 and Group 2 <u>are significantly different</u> at p < 0.05.

Summary		
	Group 1	Group 2
Mean	44.5	28.1
Variance	75.3889	72.9889
Stand. Dev.	8.6827	8.5434
n	10	10
t	3.441	
degrees of freedom	9	
critical value	2.262	

Things to remember:
If the P. Value is < than the Alpha, there is a significant difference.
If the P. Value is > than the Alpha, there is no significant difference.
If the calculated t value is > than the critical value, we reject the null Hypothesis
If the calculated t value is < than the critical value, we accept the null Hypothesis

Analysis and interpretation.
We reject the Null Hypothesis. There is a significant difference between group1 and group 2.

The Mean of group 1 is higher than group 2, hence we can observe a higher level of satisfaction in group 1 compared to group 2.

Example of Z test

A previous research shows that Filipinos consumes an average of 21 spoons of sugar per week. In disbelief, Mercy tried to disprove the statement because she believes that Filipino consume less than that. She carried out a study with 100 subjects. She obtained a Mean of 20 spoons of sugar per week with a standard deviation of 5 spoons per week. Is there a significant difference between the 2 observations?
In this question, we will use a different online calculator. (https://mathcracker.com/z-test-for-one-mean.php)

Known Values:

Mean of the hypothesis : 21 spoons of sugars / week
Sample mean: 20 spoons of sugar / week
Standard deviation of population: 5 spoons of sugar / week
Sample size = 100 subjects
Significant Level = 0.05

Hypothesis:
Null Hypothesis: Mean = 21 spoons of sugar
Alternative hypothesis: mean < 21 spoons of sugar

Then go the website calculator and fill in the blanks

Z-test for One Population Mean

Instructions: This calculator conducts a Z-test for one population mean (μ), with known population standard deviation (σ). Please select the null and alternative hypotheses, type the hypothesized mean, the significance level, the sample mean, the population standard deviation, and the sample size, and the results of the z-test will be displayed for you:

Ho: μ = ▾ μ_0

Ha: μ < ▾ μ_0

⮞ Hypothesized Mean (μ_0)	21
⮞ Sample Mean ($\bar{X}$)	20
⮞ Population St. Dev. (σ)	5
⮞ Sample Size (n)	100
⮞ Significance Level (α)	0.05

SOLVE

Then Press Solve.

Solution:

The provided sample mean is $\bar{X} = 20$ and the known population standard deviation is $\sigma = 5$, and the sample size is $n = 100$.

(1) Null and Alternative Hypotheses

The following null and alternative hypotheses need to be tested:

Ho: $\mu = 21$

Ha: $\mu < 21$

This corresponds to a left-tailed test, for which a z-test for one mean, with known population standard deviation will be used.

(2) Rejection Region

Based on the information provided, the significance level is $\alpha = 0.05$, and the critical value for a left-tailed test is $z_c = -1.64$.

The rejection region for this left-tailed test is $R = \{z : z < -1.64\}$

(3) Test Statistics

The z-statistic is computed as follows:

$$z = \frac{\bar{X} - \mu_0}{\sigma/\sqrt{n}} = \frac{20 - 21}{5/\sqrt{100}} = -2$$

(4) Decision about the null hypothesis

Since it is observed that $z = -2 < z_c = -1.64$, it is then concluded that *the null hypothesis is rejected.*

Using the P-value approach: The p-value is $p = 0.0228$, and since $p = 0.0228 < 0.05$, it is concluded that the null hypothesis is rejected.

(5) Conclusion

It is concluded that the null hypothesis Ho is *rejected*. Therefore, there is enough evidence to claim that the population mean μ is less than 21, at the 0.05 significance level.

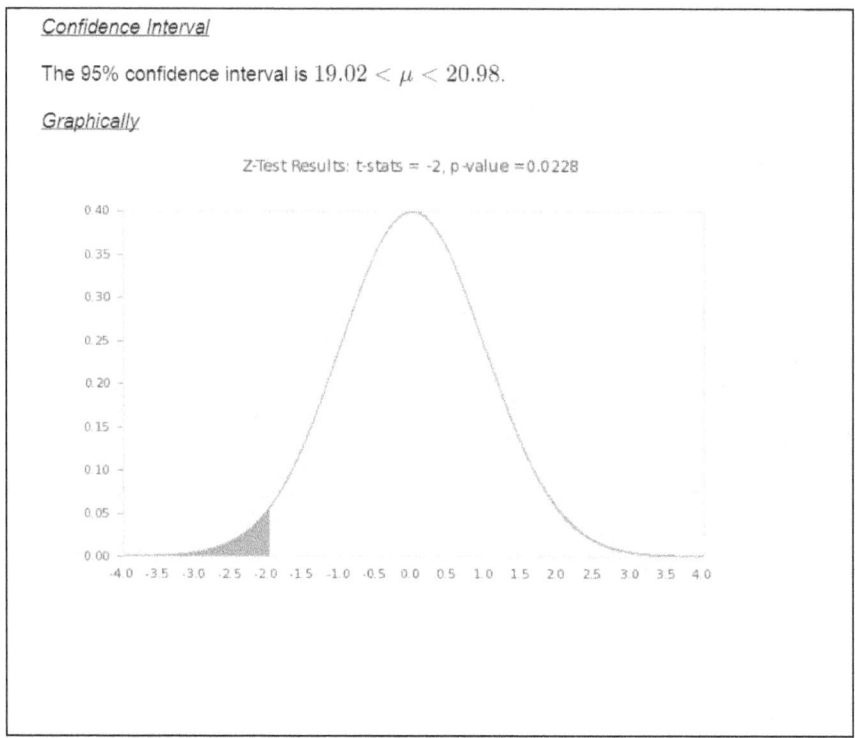

Confidence Interval

The 95% confidence interval is $19.02 < \mu < 20.98$.

Graphically

Z-Test Results: t-stats = -2, p-value = 0.0228

There are a lot more other statistical tools that can be utilized but T-test and Z-test are usually used in business hence others will be discussed in your statistics subject. By understanding and using these different calculators you can be able to do T-test and Z-test on your own. The key to statistical analysis would be to understanding what tool to use, to form your hypothesis, identifying the known value, encoding the known value to the calculator, and finally understanding the result.

Post Chapter Activity #18

Topic: Business Data Analysis

Question 1

Company PX café sold a total of 168 coffee bags on 2016.

Company NW café sold a total of 139 coffee bags on 2016.

Month	Number of coffee bags sold PX café	Number of coffee bags sold NW café
1	14	14
2	17	12
3	12	12
4	10	9
5	18	8
6	17	6
7	9	12
8	11	11
9	13	14
10	14	12
11	17	12
12	16	17
Total	n = 168 (this is the total number of sales)	n = 139

1. Find the Median of both company

2. Find the mode of both company

3. Find the mean of both company

4. Find the range of both company

5. Find the standard deviation of both company

6. Which company has a more consistent sale of coffee bag that year?

7. Using the same data set, find out if there is a significant difference in the sales of coffee bag between company PX and company NW. (alpha of 0.05)

   Null hypothesis: there is no significant difference in the sales of coffee bag between company PX and company NW.

   Alternate hypothesis: there is a significant difference in the sales of coffee bag between company PX and company NW.

Question 2

A previous research shows that Filipinos consumes an average of 70 cups of coffee per week. In disbelief, Gordon tried to validate the statement because he believes Filipino consume less than that. He carried out his own study with 100 subjects. He obtained a Mean of 65 cups of coffee per week with a standard deviation of 10 coffee per week. Is there a significant difference between the 2 observations?

Try to use (https://mathcracker.com/z-test-for-one-mean.php)

Hypothesis:

Null Hypothesis: Mean = 70 spoons of sugar

Alternative hypothesis: mean < 70 spoons of sugar

Continue to write your results here:

Lesson 18

PERA LAW

The PERA Law or (Personal Equity and Retirement account) is a personal and voluntary retirement account that motivates the regular employee's and self-employed individual to invest part of their salary or earnings for their future retirement.

Believe it or not but not a lot of people know about this law, even though it was established 2008 under the Republic Act 9505. It is a pension investment vehicle with tax perks/breaks hence it was not widely publicized.

What are these Tax perks/Breaks?

1. It gives you a 5% income tax credit. For example: if you invested Php 100,000.00 on your PERA ACCOUNT, you will get Php 5,000.00 income tax credit. So if you need to pay Php50,000.00 for your annual income tax, you only have to pay Php 45,000.00 (Php 50,000 – Php 5000 tax credit = Php 45,000)

2. It is exempted from 20% withholding tax.

3. It is exempted from 10% Dividend Tax

4. It is exempted from Capital Gain.

With all these breaks, the Government, it was estimated that the government will lose about 12 billion pesos on tax perks per year.

"We believe that the long-term benefits of the PERA would outweigh the revenue loss," said Benedict Tugonon, president of tax industry group Tax Management Association of the Philippines.

What are the 4 parties that participate in the PERA LAW?

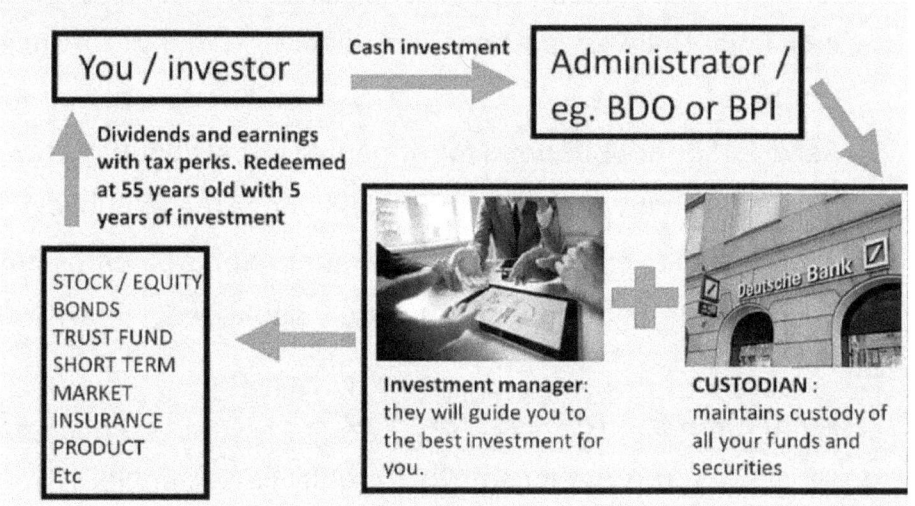

What are the 4 parties that participate in the PERA LAW?

1. **Contributor**: you can invest a maximum amount of Php100,000.00 per year for a local employee or Php200,000.00 per year for an overseas Filipino workers.

2. **Administrator**: it is either a bank (BPI and BDO) or institution that oversees the account. They have to be pre-qualified by the BSP, Insurance commission, Security exchange commission, and accredited by the Bureau of internal revenue.

3. **Investment Manager**: they will manage your investments or advise you on what is the best investment for you. They have to be accredited by the BSP, Insurance commission, and Security exchange commission.

4. **Custodian** is a separate and distinct entity unrelated to the Administrator, accredited by the BSP to take custody of PERA assets.(e.g. Deutsche Bank AG, Manila Branch for BDO)

When can you redeem income gained from PERA investment?

You can redeem it when you reach the age of 55 y/o for at least 5 years of investing. Early redemption will incur penalties.

Are there exemptions from penalties for early redemption?

Yes, if the following conditions have been observed:

1. Immediate transfer of proceeds to another Qualified/Eligible PERA investment Product and/or another Administrator within 2 working days from the withdrawal

2. For payment of accident or illness-related hospitalization in excess of thirty (30) days – needs a duly notarized doctor's certificate

3. For payment to a Contributor who has been subsequently rendered permanently totally disabled as defined under the Employees Compensation Law or Social Security System Law – needs certification from the pertinent government agency.

What do you need to invest? You have to go an administrator (BDO or BPI for now), bring your tax identification number, fill up a form and choose your investment. It's that easy

(The sources of this article was lifted from my website: Smartmoneypinoy.wixsite.com
https://smartmoneypinoy.wixsite.com/main/single-post/2017/01/16/Creating-your-wealth-thru-the-PERA-LAW)

Post Chapter Activity #19

Topic: The PERA Law

Question 1

What are the Tax advantage of the PERA Law?

Question 2

Who are parties involved in the PERA Law and what are their roles?

Question 3

What is the penalty for early redemptions?

Question 4

What is the exemption for the penalties on early redemption?

INDEX

Dr. John Michael Lao, is a medical doctor, innovator, psychologist, business strategist, business consultant, serial entrepreneur, financial advocate, researcher, financial blogger and writer, stock market investor and analyst, musician, artist, anti-poverty advocate, motivational speaker, spiritual healer, economic enthusiast, and poet. He wrote multiple award-winning Journals both in local and international events. He dedicated his medical practice to serve the poor and marginalize part of society. He believes that poverty is a disease of the mind and the cure is in increasing once financial intelligence thru financial education and empowerment.

STL

www.ingramcontent.com/pod-product-compliance
Lightning Source LLC
Chambersburg PA
CBHW070321240526
45468CB00025B/1327